elevate science

SAVVAS
LEARNING COMPANY

You are an author!

This is your book to keep. Write and draw in it! Record your data and discoveries in it! You are an author of this book!

Print your name, school, town, and state below.

My Photo

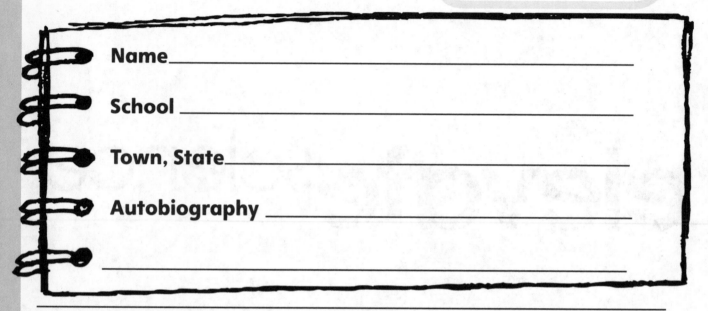

Name_____

School_____

Town, State_____

Autobiography_____

_____

SAVVAS
LEARNING COMPANY

ISBN-13: 978-0-328-94911-3
ISBN-10:   0-328-94911-6
7 2021

Program Authors

ZIPPORAH MILLER, EdD
Coordinator for K-12 Science Programs, Anne Arundel County Public Schools.
Zipporah Miller currently serves as the Senior Manager for Organizational Learning with the Anne Arundel County Public School System. Prior to that she served as the K-12 Coordinator for science in Anne Arundel County. She conducts national training to science stakeholders on the Next Generation Science Standards. Dr. Miller also served as the Associate Executive Director for Professional Development Programs and conferences at the National Science Teachers Association (NSTA) and served as a reviewer during the development of Next Generation Science Standards. Dr, Miller holds a doctoral degree from University of Maryland College Park, a master's degree in school administration and supervision from Bowie State University, and a bachelor's degree from Chadron State College.

MICHAEL J. PADILLA, PhD
Professor Emeritus, Eugene P. Moore School of Education, Clemson University, Clemson, South Carolina
Michael J. Padilla taught science in middle and secondary schools, has more than 30 years of experience educating middle grades science teachers, and served as one of the writers of the 1996 U.S. National Science Education Standards. In recent years Mike has focused on teaching science to English Language Learners. His extensive leadership experience, serving as Principal Investigator on numerous National Science Foundation and U.S. Department of Education grants, resulted in more than $35 million in funding to improve science education. He served as president of the National Science Teachers Association, the world's largest science teaching organization, in 2005–6.

MICHAEL E. WYSESSION, PhD
Professor of Earth and Planetary Sciences, Washington University, St. Louis, Missouri
An author on more than 100 science and science education publications, Dr. Wysession was awarded the prestigious National Science Foundation Presidential Faculty Fellowship and Packard Foundation Fellowship for his research in geophysics, primarily focused on using seismic tomography to determine the forces driving plate tectonics. Dr. Wysession is also a leader in geoscience literacy and education, including being chair of the Earth Science Literacy Principles, author of several popular geology Great Courses video lecture series, and a lead writer of the Next Generation Science Standards*.

---

*Next Generation Science Standards is a registered trademark of Achieve. Neither Achieve nor the lead states and partners that developed the Next Generation Science Standards were involved in the production of this product, and do not endorse it. NGSS Lead States. 2013. Next Generation Science Standards: For States, By States. Washington, DC: The National Academies Press.

Program Consultants

Carol Baker
Science Curriculum

Dr. Carol K. Baker is superintendent for Lyons Elementary K-8 School District in Lyons, Illinois. Prior to that, she was Director of Curriculum for Science and Music in Oak Lawn, Illinois. Before that she taught Physics and Earth Science for 18 years. In the recent past, Dr. Baker also wrote assessment questions for ACT (EXPLORE and PLAN), was elected president of the Illinois Science Teachers Association from 2011-2013 and served as a member of the Museum of Science and Industry advisory boards in Chicago. She is a writer of the Next Generation Science Standards. Dr. Baker received her BS in Physics and a science teaching certification. She completed her Master of Educational Administration (K-12) and earned her doctorate in Educational Leadership.

Jim Cummins
ELL

Dr. Cummins's research focuses on literacy development in multilingual schools and the role technology plays in learning across the curriculum. *Elevate Science* incorporates research-based principles for integrating language with the teaching of academic content based on Dr. Cummins's work.

Elfrieda Hiebert
Literacy

Dr. Hiebert is the President and CEO of TextProject, a nonprofit aimed at providing open-access resources for instruction of beginning and struggling readers, and a former primary school teacher. She is also a research associate at the University of California Santa Cruz. Her research addresses how fluency, vocabulary, and knowledge can be fostered through appropriate texts, and her contributions have been recognized through awards, such as the Oscar Causey Award for Outstanding Contributions to Reading Research (Literacy Research Association, 2015), Research to Practice Award (American Educational Research Association, 2013), William S. Gray Citation of Merit Award for Outstanding Contributions to Reading Research (International Reading Association, 2008).

Content Reviewers

Alex Blom, Ph.D.
Associate Professor
Department Of Physical Sciences
Alverno College
Milwaukee, Wisconsin

Joy Branlund, Ph.D.
Department of Physical Science
Southwestern Illinois College
Granite City, Illinois

Judy Calhoun
Associate Professor
Physical Sciences
Alverno College
Milwaukee, Wisconsin

Stefan Debbert
Associate Professor of Chemistry
Lawrence University
Appleton, Wisconsin

Diane Doser
Professor
Department of Geological Sciences
University of Texas at El Paso
El Paso, Texas

Rick Duhrkopf, Ph. D.
Department of Biology
Baylor University
Waco, Texas

Jennifer Liang
University Of Minnesota Duluth
Duluth, Minnesota

Heather Mernitz, Ph.D.
Associate Professor of Physical Sciences
Alverno College
Milwaukee, Wisconsin

Joseph McCullough, Ph.D.
Cabrillo College
Aptos, California

Katie M. Nemeth, Ph.D.
Assistant Professor
College of Science and Engineering
University of Minnesota Duluth
Duluth, Minnesota

Maik Pertermann
Department of Geology
Western Wyoming Community College
Rock Springs, Wyoming

Scott Rochette
Department of the Earth Sciences
The College at Brockport
 State University of New York
Brockport, New York

David Schuster
Washington University in St Louis
St. Louis, Missouri

Shannon Stevenson
Department of Biology
University of Minnesota Duluth
Duluth, Minnesota

Paul Stoddard, Ph.D.
Department of Geology and
 Environmental Geosciences
Northern Illinois University
DeKalb, Illinois

Nancy Taylor
American Public University
Charles Town, West Virginia

Safety Reviewers

Douglas Mandt, M.S.
Science Education Consultant
Edgewood, Washington

Juliana Textley, Ph.D.
Author, NSTA books on school
 science safety
Adjunct Professor
Lesley University
Cambridge, Massachusetts

Teacher Reviewers

Jennifer Bennett, M.A.
Memorial Middle School
Tampa, Florida

Sonia Blackstone
Lake County Schools
Howey In the Hills, Florida

Teresa Bode
Roosevelt Elementary
Tampa, Florida

Tyler C. Britt, Ed.S.
Curriculum & Instructional
 Practice Coordinator
Raytown Quality Schools
Raytown, Missouri

A. Colleen Campos
Grandview High School
Aurora, Colorado

Ronald Davis
Riverview Elementary
Riverview, Florida

Coleen Doulk
Challenger School
Spring Hill, Florida

Mary D. Dube
Burnett Middle School
Seffner, Florida

Sandra Galpin
Adams Middle School
Tampa, Florida

Rhonda Graham
Science Supervisor
Pittsburgh Public Schools
Pittsburgh, Pennsylvania

Margaret Henry
Lebanon Junior High School
Lebanon, Ohio

Christina Hill
Beth Shields Middle School
Ruskin, Florida

Judy Johnis
Gorden Burnett Middle School
Seffner, Florida

Karen Y. Johnson
Beth Shields Middle School
Ruskin, Florida

Jane Kemp
Lockhart Elementary School
Tampa, Florida

Denise Kuhling
Adams Middle School
Tampa, Florida

Esther Leonard M.Ed. and L.M.T.
Gifted and Talented Implementation Specialist
San Antonio Independent School District
San Antonio, Texas

Kelly Maharaj
Science Department Chairperson
Challenger K8 School of Science and
 Mathematics
Elgin, Florida

Kevin J. Maser, Ed.D.
H. Frank Carey Jr/Sr High School
Franklin Square, New York

Angie L. Matamoros, Ph.D.
ALM Science Consultant
Weston, Florida

Corey Mayle
Brogden Middle School
Durham, North Carolina

Keith McCarthy
George Washington Middle School
Wayne, New Jersey

Yolanda O. Peña
John F. Kennedy Junior High School
West Valley City, Utah

Kathleen M. Poe
Jacksonville Beach Elementary School
Jacksonville Beach, Florida

Wendy Rauld
Monroe Middle School
Tampa, Florida

Anne Rice
Woodland Middle School
Gurnee, Illinois

Pat (Patricia) Shane, Ph.D.
STEM & ELA Education Consultant
Chapel Hill, North Carolina

Diana Shelton
Burnett Middle School
Seffner, Florida

Nakia Sturrup
Jennings Middle School
Seffner, Florida

Melissa Triebwasser
Walden Lake Elementary
Plant City, Florida

Michele Bubley Wiehagen
Science Coach
Miles Elementary School
Tampa, Florida

Pauline Wilcox
Instructional Science Coach
Fox Chapel Middle School
Spring Hill, Florida

Sky and Earth

Quest

In this Quest activity, you meet a space scientist. She needs your help. She wants you to find a way to tell students about patterns in the sky.

Like the space scientist, you will complete activities and labs. You will use what you learn in the lessons to write a play about sky patterns.

Find your Quest activities on pages 11, 18, and 24.

Career Connection Space Scientist on page 29

- VIDEO
- eTEXT
- INTERACTIVITY
- SCIENCE SONG
- GAME
- DOCUMENT
- ASSESSMENT

The Essential Question

HANDS-ON LAB

Topic 2

Earth's Surface

SC.1.E.6.1, SC.1.E.6.2, SC.1.E.6.3

- ▶ VIDEO
- 📖 eTEXT
- 👆 INTERACTIVITY
- ▶ SCIENCE SONG
- 🎮 GAME
- 📄 DOCUMENT
- ☑ ASSESSMENT

Quest

In this Quest activity, you meet a geologist. He needs your help. He would like you to show other students how land and water change along a river.

Like the geologist, you will complete activities and labs. You will use what you learn in the lessons to make a scrapbook about land and water along a river.

Find your Quest activities on pages 47, 54, and 62.

Career Connection Geologist on page 65

The Essential Question

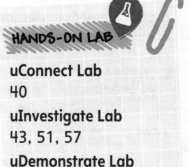

HANDS-ON LAB

Matter and Movement

 SC.1.P.8.1, SC.1.P.12.1, SC.1.P.13.1

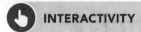 VIDEO

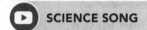 eTEXT

 INTERACTIVITY

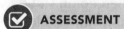 SCIENCE SONG

 GAME

 DOCUMENT

ASSESSMENT

Quest

In this **STEM** Quest activity, you meet a mechanical engineer. He has a problem for you to solve. You need to design a machine. The machine must send supplies from a boat to land.

Like the mechanical engineer, you will complete activities and labs. You will use what you learn in the lessons to design and build a catapult.

Find your Quest activities on pages 83, 88, and 98

Career Connection Mechanical Engineer on page 101

HANDS-ON LAB

Topic 4
Living Things

Quest

In this **STEM** Quest activity, you meet a bioengineer. She wants you to think of a problem people have. Then you will find a way to use a plant or animal part to help solve the problem.

Like the bioengineer, you will complete activities and labs. Use what you learn in the lessons to find a plant or animal part that will help solve a human problem.

Find your Quest activities on pages 119, 125, 131, 138, and 146

Career Connection Bioengineer on page 149

SC.1.L.14.1, SC.1.L.14.2, SC.1.L.14.3, SC.1.L.17.1

▶ VIDEO

📖 eTEXT

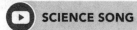
👆 INTERACTIVITY

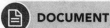
▶ SCIENCE SONG

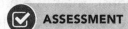
🎮 GAME

📄 DOCUMENT

☑ ASSESSMENT

HANDS-ON LAB

Parents and Offspring

Quest

In this Quest activity, you meet a nature scientist. She has a problem. Some animals have escaped from the zoo. Help her find the parents of three young animals.

Like the nature scientist, you will complete activities and labs. You will use what you learn in the lessons to match the adult animals with their young. Then you will make a model of an adult and young animal.

Find your Quest activities on pages 166, 175, and 186

Career Connection nature scientist on page 189

 VIDEO

 eTEXT

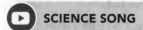 INTERACTIVITY

 SCIENCE SONG

 GAME

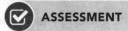 DOCUMENT

ASSESSMENT

The Essential Question

HANDS-ON LAB

Go to **SavvasRealize.com** to access your digital course.

Elevate Science combines the best science writing with a robust online program. Throughout the lessons, look for digital support to increase your learning experience.

Online Resources

Savvas Realize™ is your online science class. It includes:

- Student eTEXT
- Teacher eTEXT
- Project-Based Learning
- Labs

- Interactivities
- Videos
- Assessments
- Study Tools
- and more!

Digital Features

 VIDEO

 INTERACTIVITY

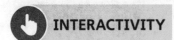 LAB

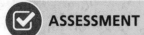 ASSESSMENT

 eTEXT

 GAME

SONG

Look for these **symbols**. They tell you that there are more things to do and learn online.

 INTERACTIVITY

Compare how living things and their parents are alike and different.

Elevate your thinking!

Elevate Science for Florida takes science to a whole new level and lets you take ownership of your learning. Explore science in the world around you. Investigate how things work. Think critically and solve problems! *Elevate Science* helps you think like a scientist, so you're ready for a world of discoveries.

Explore Your World

Explore real-life scenarios with engaging Quests that dig into science topics in Florida and around the world. You can:

- Solve real-world problems
- Apply skills and knowledge
- Communicate solutions

Quest Kickoff

Find the Parents

What clues help us find a young animal's parent?

Make Connections

Elevate Science connects science to other subjects and shows you how to better understand the world through:

- Mathematics
- Reading and Writing
- Literacy

Literacy ▸ Toolbox

Main Ideas and Details All living things grow and change is the main idea. Use the details to tell how a watermelon plant changes during its life cycle.  LAFS.1.RI.1.2

Math ▸ Toolbox

Compare Numbers You can compare how long objects are. Parent rabbits have longer ears than young rabbits. Use cubes to measure the lengths of two classroom objects. Which is longer?

 MAFS.1.MD.1.1

Connecting Concepts ▸ Toolbox

Patterns Nature has many patterns. A **pattern** is something that repeats. Parents protect their young. They use their bodies to protect them. What patterns do you see on these two pages?

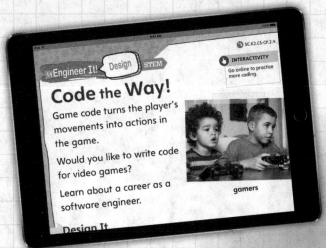

Build Skills for the Future

- Master the Engineering Design Process
- Apply critical thinking and analytical skills
- Learn about STEM careers

Focus on Reading Skills

Elevate Science creates ongoing reading connections to help you develop the reading skills you need to succeed. Features include:

- Leveled Readers
- Literacy Connection Features
- Reading Checks

Literacy Connection

LAFS.1.RI.1.2

Main Idea and Details

Nature scientists observe animals. Read about the main idea and details of geese and their young.

The main idea is what the sentences are about. Details tell about the main idea.

GAME
Practice what you learn with the Toolbox Games.

Enter the Lab Zone

Hands-on experiments and virtual labs help you test ideas and show what you know in performance-based assessments. Scaffolded labs include:

- STEM Labs
- Design Your Own
- Open-ended Labs

Explore the Next Generation Sunshine State Science Standards for:

- Connecting Concepts to make connections
- Nature of Science standards to build inquiry skills
- Big Ideas, Benchmarks, and standards to master content

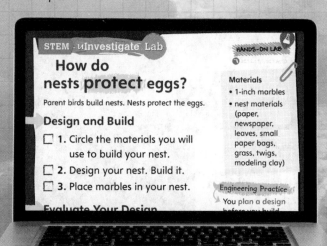

Engineering Practice
You plan a design before you build something.

⚠ Wash your hands when you are done.

Sky and Earth

SC.1.E.5.1 Observe and discuss that there are more stars in the sky than anyone can easily count and that they are not scattered evenly in the sky. **SC.1.E.5.2** Explore the Law of Gravity by demonstrating that Earth's gravity pulls any object on or near Earth toward it even though nothing is touching the object. **SC.1.E.5.3** Investigate how magnifiers make things appear bigger and help people see things they could not see without them. **SC.1.E.5.4** Identify the beneficial and harmful properties of the Sun. (Also **SC.1.N.1.1, SC.1.N.1.3, LAFS.1.RI.3.7, MAFS.1.G.1.3**, and **MAFS.1.OA.3.5**)

Go online to access
your digital course.

 VIDEO

 eTEXT

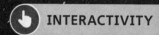 INTERACTIVITY

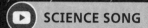 SCIENCE SONG

 GAME

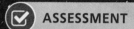 ASSESSMENT

The Essential Question What objects are in the sky, and how do they move?

Show What You Know

What do people see in the sky when they look through a telescope? How does a telescope change how objects in the sky look? Tell a partner.

Sky Watchers

What patterns can you see in the sky?

Hi! My name is Ms. Collins. I am a space scientist. I heard some students talking about the night sky. One student said, "I saw a round moon. There were too many stars to count!" Another student said, "I saw a moon that looked like a smile. There were only a few stars!" A third student said, "I can't see the moon on some nights!"

All the students were right! How can that be? Help me explain patterns in the sky to the students. The path shows the Quest activities you will complete as you work through the topic. Check off your progress each time you complete an activity with a

QUEST CHECK ✓ OFF .

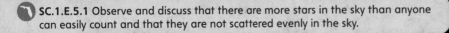

SC.1.E.5.1 Observe and discuss that there are more stars in the sky than anyone can easily count and that they are not scattered evenly in the sky.

▶ **VIDEO**

Watch a video about a space scientist.

Quest Check-In Lab 3

Lesson 3

Model how Earth moves.

Quest Check-In 2

Lesson 2

Tell which picture shows what you see through a telescope.

Quest Findings

Complete the Quest! Find a fun way to show patterns in the sky.

Quest Check-In 1

Lesson 1

Tell how stars look in the sky.

Which way will it point?

Space scientists need to study forces.
How can you study one of these forces?

Procedure

Materials
- paper clip
- string
- pencil
- table

☐ **1.** Find a way to use the materials to make the paper clip hang down.

☐ **2.** Try to make the paper clip hang on its side. Predict what you think will happen.

_____

_____

_____

_____

Analyze and Interpret Data

3. Did what you see support your prediction? Why or why not?

_____

_____

4. What might happen if you move the paper clip off the desk with nothing to hold it up?

_____

_____

Picture Clues

LAFS.1.RI.3.7

GAME

Practice what you learn with the Mini Games.

Space scientists study pictures of space to find patterns. What can you learn by studying a picture?

Pictures are like clues. They can help you figure out what you are reading. They can help you learn more about the text. Read the text below, then look at the picture.

Seeing Earth

Look out the window. Can you see all of Earth? We cannot see all of Earth from one place. Spacecraft move around Earth. They can take pictures of Earth from space. The pictures help us see all of Earth.

☑ **Reading Check** Picture Clues Tell what the picture shows. Tell one thing you learned from this picture.

Observe the Sky

 VIDEO

Watch a video about stars.

SC.1.E.5.1 Observe and discuss that there are more stars in the sky than anyone can easily count and that they are not scattered evenly in the sky. **SC.1.E.5.2** Explore the Law of Gravity by demonstrating that Earth's gravity pulls any object on or near Earth toward it even though nothing is touching the object. **SC.1.E.5.4** Identify the beneficial and harmful properties of the Sun. (Also **SC.1.N.1.1** and **LAFS.1.RI.3.7**)

Vocabulary

star

sun

gravity

I can describe the sun, the moon, and the stars.

Jumpstart Discovery!

What do you see in the day sky? Draw it on a sheet of paper. Then draw what you see in the night sky. Tell how your drawings are alike and different.

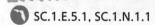
Why is it hard to see stars during the day?

Material
• flashlight

On clear nights, you can see many stars in the sky. Why can we only see the sun during the day?

Procedure

☐ **1.** Make a plan to **model** a star in the night sky and day sky. Use the flashlight.

☐ **2.** Show your plan to your teacher before you start.

☐ **3.** Record your observations.

night	day

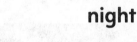

Analyze and Interpret Data

4. Explain Why can you see the sun but no other stars during the day?

_____

_____

_____

Star Light, Star Bright

A **star** is a big ball of hot gas. Stars look small because they are far from us.

Stars are seen at night. You cannot see most stars in the day.

Have you ever tried to count all the stars in the sky? There are too many stars to count!

Draw Conclusions Look at the night sky. Tell a partner how easy it is to count the stars. Tell how the stars are scattered all over the sky.

Literacy ▸ Toolbox

Picture Clues Is it daytime or nighttime in the small picture? Tell how you know.

LAFS.1.RI.3.7

The Sun, Our Star

You can see only one star in the day. The sun is a star.

The **sun** is the closest star to Earth. This is why it looks bigger and brighter than other stars. We cannot live without heat and light from the sun.

The sun can also harm living things. It can give you a sunburn.

Identify Underline one way the sun is helpful. Circle one way the sun is harmful.

Quest Connection

When can you see many stars? When can you only see the sun? Describe the pattern to a partner.

Gravity and the Moon

Gravity is a force, like a pull. It pulls objects toward one another. Gravity pulls objects to the center of Earth. It makes a ball fall to the ground. It keeps you from floating into space.

The moon is the closest large object to Earth in space. Gravity keeps the moon close to Earth.

Explain Nothing is touching these paper planes. Draw an arrow to show how Earth's gravity will affect them. Tell a partner why this will happen. Test paper planes in your class to see if you were correct.

Stars in the Sky

Look at the pictures.

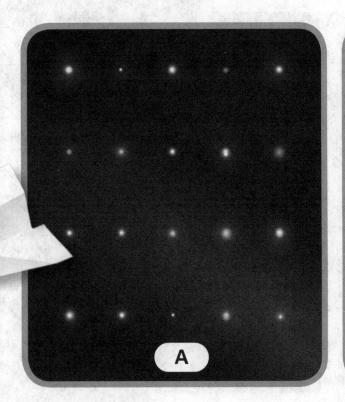

A

B

1. Circle the picture that shows the way stars appear in the sky.

2. Why did you choose this picture?

_____

- -

_____

_____

- -

_____

VIDEO

Watch a video about Earth's rotation.

SC.1.E.5.3 Investigate how magnifiers make things appear bigger and help people see things they could not see without them. (Also **SC.1.N.1.1**, **SC.1.N.1.3**, **MAFS.1.G.1.3**, and **MAFS.1.OA.3.5**)

Lesson 2

Patterns in the Sky

I can tell what causes day and night and moon phases.

Vocabulary

rotation

sunrise

sunset

moon phase

Jumpstart Discovery!

How many different shapes of the moon have you seen? Draw the shapes on a sheet of paper. Cut out the shapes. Put the shapes on a night sky poster.

uInvestigate Lab

How can you observe sun patterns?

Space scientists study the sun during the day. What patterns can you see in the day sky?

Procedure

☐ **1.** Make a plan to **observe** sun patterns throughout the day.

☐ **2.** Show your plan to your teacher.

☐ **3.** Make your observations. Draw them.

Science Practice

You **observe** to look for patterns.

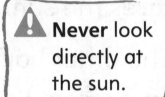 **Never** look directly at the sun.

Analyze and Interpret Data

4. Explain How does the sun seem to move in a pattern during the day?

_____

_____

_____

Earth Spins

Earth spins in space. It makes one spin every 24 hours. This motion is called **rotation**.

Rotation causes day and night. As Earth spins, one half of Earth faces the sun. It is daytime there.

The other half of Earth faces away from the sun. It is nighttime there.

sunrise

Identify Make a small **X** on the picture of Earth. Tell whether it is day or night at that place.

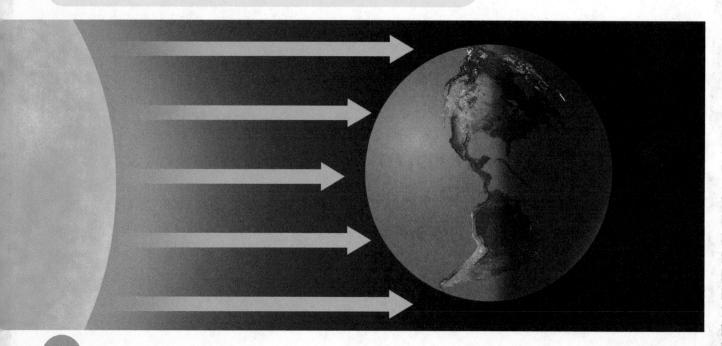

Sunrise, Sunset

Sunrise happens when the sun seems to rise in the morning. Then the sun seems to move across the sky. It is high in the sky around noon.

Sunset happens when the sun seems to set in the evening. The sun is not moving. The rotation of Earth makes the sun seem to move. It makes the moon seem to rise and set, too.

sunset

Explain What makes the sun seem to move? Fill in the box.

Cause	Effect
	The sun seems to move.

Moon Motions and Phases

The moon moves in a path around Earth. It takes the moon a little less than a month to go around Earth. The moon spins just like Earth does.

The sun shines on the moon. This makes the moon bright at night.

The moon seems to change shape. As the moon moves around Earth, the amount of sun that shines on it changes. The changing shapes of the moon are called **moon phases**.

A Closer View

Would you like to see the moon or stars up close? A telescope is a tool that makes things look bigger.

You can use a telescope to see the sky. The moon looks bigger. You can see more stars in the sky.

Never look at the sun with this tool. You could hurt your eyes.

INTERACTIVITY

Go online to explore patterns in the night sky.

☑ Reading Check **Picture Clues**
How do you use a telescope? Look at the picture for clues.

Quest Connection

▼▼▼▼▼▼▼▼▼▼▼▼▼▼▼▼▼▼▼▼▼▼▼▼▼▼

What can space scientists learn by using telescopes to look at the sky? Tell a partner.

Moon Patterns

Look at the pictures.
They show the full moon.

Think about the phases of the moon. What do they tell you about how the moon moves around Earth?

Put a small **X** on the full moon you would see through a telescope. What details can you see on this full moon that you cannot see on the other? Why?

_____

_____

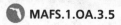

MAFS.1.OA.3.5

Use a Calendar

The moon goes through phases. The moon takes 29 days to go through all its phases. You can predict the next full moon.

Sun	Mon	Tue	Wed	Thu	Fri	Sat
				1	2	3
4	5	6	7	8	9	10
11	12	13	14	15	16	17
18	19	20	21	22	23	24
25	26	27	28	29	30	31

Find the full moon. What is the date of the full moon? Predict the date of the next full moon.

Draw the next full moon on the calendar.

Lesson 3

Daylight Changes and Seasons

 VIDEO

Watch the video to learn about about sun patterns in different seasons.

INTERACTIVITY

Go online to learn more about the seasons.

SC.1.N.1.1, SC.1.N.1.3, and MAFS.1.OA.1.1

Vocabulary

season

I can explain why days have different lengths during different seasons.

Jumpstart Discovery!

Act out something you like to do in your favorite season. Have a partner guess your favorite season.

How does the sun cause seasons?

In many places, seasons change. How can you model seasons?

Materials
- balloon
- marker
- light source

Procedure

☐ **1.** Use the materials to **model** how sunlight hits Earth. Make a plan to collect data at three spots on your model Earth.

Science Practice
You **use models** to show what something is like.

☐ **2.** Show your plan to your teacher.

☐ **3.** Think of a way to change how light hits your model of Earth as it moves around the model sun. Record your observations.

Analyze and Interpret Data

4. Explain What happened to light on your model of Earth? Tell a partner.

Seasons

Earth moves around the sun. Earth makes one path around the sun in 365 days.

As Earth moves, sunlight hits parts of Earth differently. These patterns can be predicted. This causes seasons. **Seasons** are summer, fall, winter, and spring.

Visual Literacy Which season are you having now? Circle the picture.

Quest Connection

What patterns in the amount of daylight do you observe as Earth moves around the Sun? Tell a partner.

In summer, your part of Earth gets a lot of sunshine. Daylight hours are long. Summer is warm.

In fall, your part of Earth gets a little less sunshine. Daylight hours get shorter. Fall is cool.

In spring, your part of Earth begins to get more sunshine. Daylight hours get longer. Spring is cool.

In winter, your part of Earth gets the least amount of sunshine. Daylight hours are short. Winter is cold. Draw something you see in winter.

How can you model the motions of Earth?

Earth spins once every day. It moves around the sun in one year. How can you model these motions? How can you show what the motions cause?

Materials

- construction paper
- flashlight
- drawing materials

Procedure

☐ **1.** In your group, decide who will be the models for different objects in the sky.

☐ **2.** Plan how your models will work.

☐ **3.** Show your teacher your plan.

☐ **4.** **Model** one pattern caused by the rotation of Earth. Explain how your model works.

_____

_____

_____

_____

_____

Analyze and Interpret Data

4. Describe What patterns did you model?

_____

_____

_____

5. Connect How could you model seasons?

_____

_____

_____

6. Draw Conclusions How do movements of Earth change how we live?

_____

_____

_____

Design a Code

Earth takes one year to move around the sun. There are 12 months in a year. How can you make a code to tell where Earth is each month?

VIDEO

Watch a video about how Earth revolves around the sun.

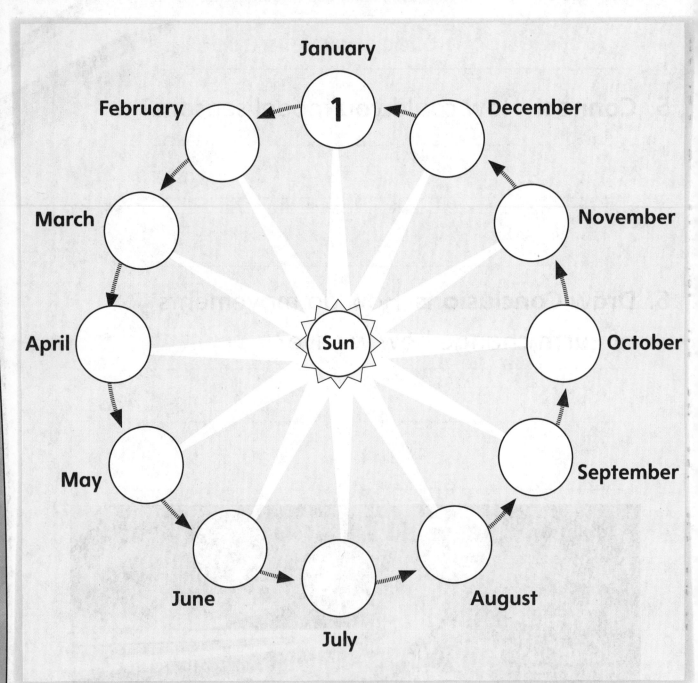

Design It

The picture shows Earth moving around the sun. Position 1 is Earth in January. Each circle stands for a different month.

☐ **1.** Design a code that tells about Earth's position around the sun each month.

☐ **2.** Write four months of your code here.

_____ _____

_____ _____

_____ _____

☐ **3.** Share your code. Tell how it works.

_____

_____

_____

☐ **4.** See if your code works. Use a code number to describe the position of Earth. Your partner should tell you what month it is.

👆 INTERACTIVITY

Go online for ideas for your play about sky patterns.

Sky Watchers

What patterns can you see in the sky?

Look back through the pages. How many patterns can you find? Draw a pattern you see.

Show What You Found

Work in a group. Write a play that shows patterns in the sky. You can use drawings in your play. You can use photos. People can be the sun, the moon, the stars, and Earth. Use your play to describe and predict patterns based on your observations of the sun, moon, and stars.

Space Scientist

Space scientists study objects in space. They observe the sun and moon. They study Earth, too. Space scientists use telescopes. They study pictures taken by spacecraft.

Some space scientists travel in space. They live in spacecraft that move around Earth. Do you see the floating objects in the top image? There is very little gravity in space. The space scientists float, too.

What object in the sky would you like to study?

_____

_____

_____

 **Assessment**

The Essential Question **What objects are in the sky, and how do they move?**

Show What You Learned
Tell a partner what you learned about how objects in the sky move.

Read each question and choose or write the best answer.

1. What does the picture show?
   a. a phase of the moon
   b. the rotation of Earth
   c. a cause of seasons
   d. the rising of the sun

2. Draw two pictures of you. The first picture should show how gravity affects you. The second picture should show what would happen without gravity.

3. Describe how hours of daylight change with the seasons. Use the word bank to fill in the table.

| winter | more | fewer | summer |

Season	Hours of Daylight

4. Which sentence best describes stars?
   a. Stars are close to Earth.
   b. Stars give off light and heat.
   c. We see stars during the day.
   d. Stars are spaced evenly in the sky.

Read the scenario and answer questions 1–2.

Fiona drew a model of stars in the sky.

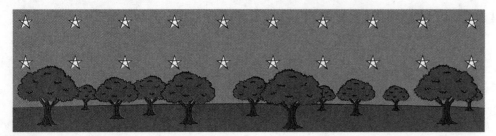

1 How can Fiona improve her model?

Ⓐ Fiona can show that stars are scattered.

Ⓑ Fiona can show the sun.

Ⓒ Fiona can show stars in the day sky.

Ⓓ Fiona can show stars that are the same size.

2 Benjamin claims that a telescope can help Fiona observe stars in the night sky. Which statement **best** supports his claim?

Ⓕ Telescopes make stars look farther away.

Ⓖ Telescopes make stars look smaller.

Ⓗ Telescopes make stars look darker.

Ⓘ Telescopes make stars look closer and bigger.

Read the scenario and answer questions 3–4.

Kate made a model of how Earth moves. First, she made the ball spin in front of the lamp. Then she moved the ball in a circle, or path, around the lamp.

3 What did Kate model first?

Ⓐ She modeled phases of the sun.

Ⓑ She modeled sunrises.

Ⓒ She modeled Earth's rotation.

Ⓓ She modeled sunsets.

4 What did the ball's path around the lamp show?

Ⓕ the moon's rotation

Ⓖ the moon's path around Earth

Ⓗ Earth's rotation

Ⓘ Earth's path around the sun

How do shadows change?

Earth's movement causes shadows from the sun in patterns that can be predicted. How can you observe these patterns?

Materials
- wood stick
- ruler

Procedure

☐ **1.** Predict if a shadow stays the same during the day.

☐ **2.** Make a plan to test your prediction. Use all the materials. Remember to take measurements.

☐ **3.** Show your plan to your teacher before you begin.

☐ **4.** Make **your observations**.

Observations

	Length of shadow	How the pattern changed
Observation 1		
Observation 2		
Observation 3		

Analyze and Interpret Data

5. Interpret What happened to the shadow?

_____

_____

_____

_____

6. Explain What pattern do your observations show?

_____

_____

_____

_____

Earth's Surface

SC.1.E.5.3 Investigate how magnifiers make things appear bigger and help people see things they could not see without them. **SC.1.E.6.1** Recognize that water, rocks, soil, and living organisms are found on Earth's surface., **SC.1.E.6.2** Describe the need for water and how to be safe around water., **SC.1.E.6.3** Recognize that some things in the world around us happen fast and some happen slowly. (Also **SC.L.1.14.3, SC.2.L.17.1, SC.1.N.1.1, SC.1.N.1.2, SC.1.N.1.3, SC.1.N.1.4, LAFS.K12.R.1.1, MAFS.1.MD.3**)

The Essential Question What can you tell about Earth's surface?

Show What You Know

Compare the photos.
Tell a partner what
you see.

Mystery Along the River

What clues show how Earth's surface changes?

Hi! My name is Mr. Garcia. I am a geologist. I study the land and water on Earth.

I went on a rafting trip. I took these pictures. Notice the landforms and plants. Can you help me? I need to describe how the plants and landforms can be so different along the same river. Look for clues in the pictures and text as you read. The path shows the Quest activities you will complete as you work through the topic. Check off your progress each time you complete an activity with a **QUEST CHECK ✓ OFF** .

SC.1.E.6.1 Recognize that water, rocks, soil, and living organisms are found on Earth's surface. **SC.1.E.6.3** Recognize that some things in the world around us happen fast and some happen slowly.

Quest Check-In 1

Lesson 1 ■
Compare soil and plants along a river.

Quest Check-In 2

Lesson 2 ●
Observe how water moves along a river.

Quest Check-In Lab 3

Lesson 3 ◆
Compare changes to land along a river.

Quest Findings

Complete the Quest! Draw pictures of the photos. Write captions.

What is in the dirt?

Geologists can observe dirt with a hand lens. A hand lens makes small objects appear larger. What observations can you make about dirt?

Materials

- hand lens
- paper
- dirt

Procedure

☐ **1.** Use your hand lens. Observe the dirt.

☐ **2.** Draw what you see. Label your work.

 Please wash your hands thoroughly after touching the sample.

Analyze and Interpret Data

3. Tell Look at your drawing. Put an "X" on the living things.

4. Ask Share questions you have about what you found in the dirt.

Draw Conclusions

Geologists and miners sometimes work together. Read about what they do.

Add clues from the text to what you know to draw a conclusion.

GAME

Practice what you learn with the Mini Games.

Geologists and Miners

Geologists find places where rocks are buried. Miners drill or dig into the rock. They drill deep under the ground for oil. Some miners dig for coal, iron, or even diamonds.

☑ Reading Check Draw Conclusions

Underline words that show why geologists and miners can work together. Tell how you know.

Rocks and Soil

SC.1.E.5.3 Investigate how magnifiers make things appear bigger and help people see things they could not see without them. SC.1.E.6.1 Recognize that water, rocks, soil, and living organisms are found on Earth's surface. (Also SC.1.L.14.3, SC.1.N.1.1, SC.1.N.1.2, and LAFS.K12.R.1.1)

Vocabulary

mineral

soil

I can observe that rocks, soil, land, water, and living things are found on Earth's surface.

Jumpstart Discovery!

Tell a partner what you know about rocks. Name two objects made from rock. Where do you find rock every day?

What are the properties of rocks?

HANDS-ON LAB

SC.1.E.5.3, SC.1.E.6.1, SC.1.N.1.2

Geologists observe rocks. How can you observe rocks?

Materials
• hand lens
• rocks

Procedure

☑ **1.** Look at the rocks. Think of a way to **observe** them.

☑ **2.** Draw and describe your observations of the rocks.

☑ **3.** Use words to describe their properties.

Science Practice

When you use your senses, you **observe**.

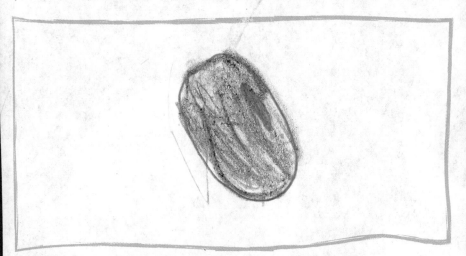

Analyze and Interpret Data

4. Compare your drawings with others. Tell what you notice.

Rocks

Look at Earth's surface. You can see grass, plants, and animals. You can see mountains and water. Below the ground, the surface of Earth is made of rock. Rocks are hard, solid parts of Earth. They are found in many sizes. Some are huge! Some are tiny.

Label the rocks and minerals in the pictures with the words below.

~~colorful~~ ~~dull~~ striped brown

colorful

dull

Minerals

Rocks are made of **minerals.** Minerals make up Earth's rocks and sands. Minerals are nonliving things. They do not come from plants and animals. Minerals give rocks their colors and their hardness.

👆 **INTERACTIVITY**

Go online to learn more about the features of Earth's surface.

Striped brown

Quest Connection

Tell where rocks can be found.

Soil

Soil is loose material that covers the surface of Earth. Plants grow in soil. Some animals live in soil. Soil contains living and nonliving things like bits of rocks, water, gases, leaves, and small animals.

There are many kinds of soil. Some plants live in rich, dark soil. Other plants can live in sandy soil. Still other plants can live in rocky soil or in clay soil.

Recognize Tell what living and nonliving things can be found on Earth's surface.

Literacy ▸ Toolbox

Draw Conclusions
Draw a conclusion. Explain why soil is an important part of Earth's surface.

 LAFS.K12.R.1.1

Plants and Animals Need Soil

Look at Mr. Garcia's photos below. Compare the plants. Compare the types of soil the plants grow in. Fill in the labels for each type of soil.

Use the drawing space to draw a picture of the plants and soil near your school. Label your drawing.

SC.1.E.6.1, SC.1.N.1.1

☝ **INTERACTIVITY**

Go online to learn about maps that geologists use.

Map It Out

Geologists use maps. Most maps are flat. Some kinds of maps show where land is raised up.

Suwannee River Hiking Trail

Model It

A map is a model. You can also use maps to make other models.

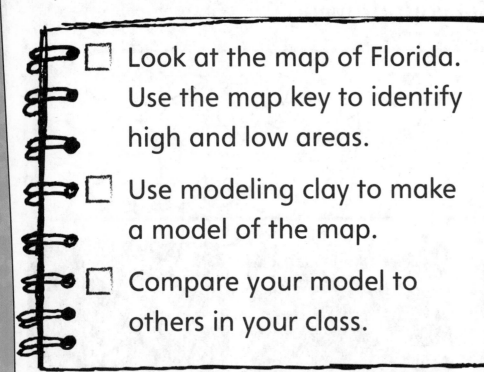

- ☐ Look at the map of Florida. Use the map key to identify high and low areas.

- ☐ Use modeling clay to make a model of the map.

- ☐ Compare your model to others in your class.

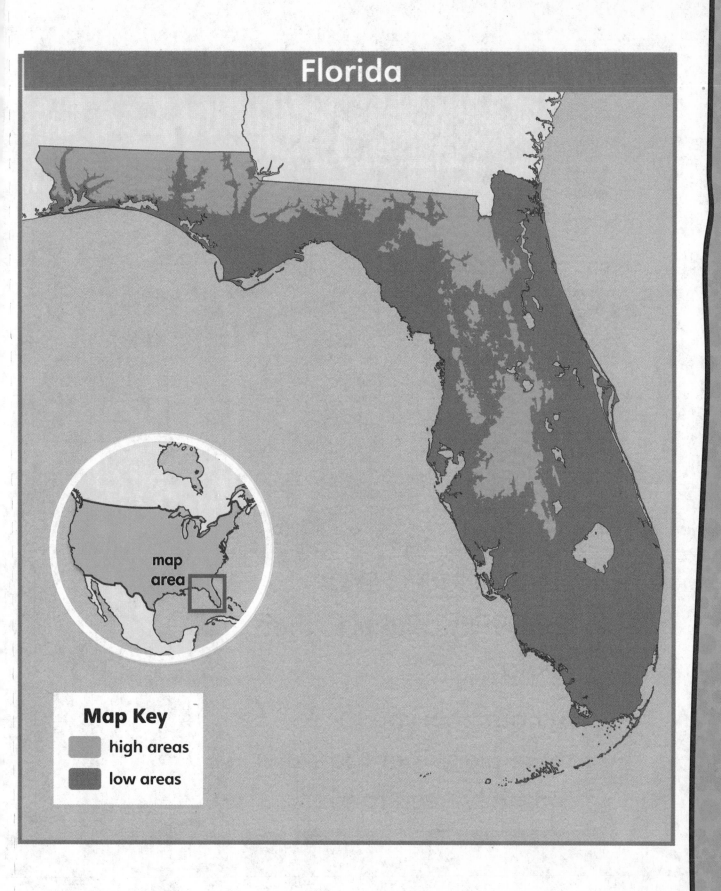

Florida

Map Key
- high areas
- low areas

map area

Water on Earth

SC.1.E.6.1 Recognize that water, rocks, soil, and living organisms are found on Earth's surface., SC.1.E.6.2 Describe the need for water and how to be safe around water., SC.1.E.6.3 Recognize that some things in the world around us happen fast and some happen slowly.(Also SC.1.N.1.2 and MAFS.1.MD.3)

Vocabulary

ocean

I can explain where water is found on Earth.

I can describe how to be safe around water.

Jumpstart Discovery!

Look at the plants in the photo.

Act out how you think these plants get the water that they need to live.

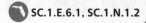
How do plants get water?

Scientists observe what living things need. How do plants get water? How can you observe it?

Materials

- 2 white flowers
- 2 plastic cups
- water
- food coloring

Procedure

☐ **1.** Make a plan to show how water moves through plants. Use all of the materials.

☐ **2.** Tell your plan to your teacher.

☐ **3.** **Observe** the flowers for two days. Record your observations.

Science Practice

You **observe** to find out more information about something.

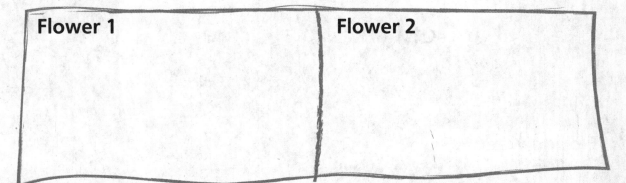

Flower 1	Flower 2

Analyze and Interpret Data

4. **Tell** Explain what happened to the flowers.

Water on Earth

Most water on Earth is in the ocean. The **ocean** is the large body of salt water that covers almost three-fourths of the surface of Earth.

Water can also be found in rivers, lakes, streams, and ponds. Living things need water. Many living things live in water.

Math ▸ Toolbox

Pie Chart This pie chart shows how people use fresh water. How do you use water? How can you save water?

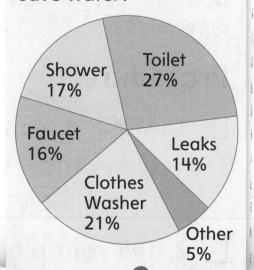

Shower 17%
Toilet 27%
Faucet 16%
Leaks 14%
Clothes Washer 21%
Other 5%

MAFS.1.MD.3

Florida wetlands

Water Safety

INTERACTIVITY

Go online to learn more about the water on Earth's surface.

Living things use water. People and animals use water to bathe, swim, and play.

Be safe around water. Always have an adult with you while you swim. Do not run when you are near a pool.

Describe Work with a partner. Describe how you stay safe around water.

_____

_____

_____

_____

Quest Connection

The Quest pictures were taken along a river. Tell where else water is found on Earth's surface.

How Rivers Flow

Rivers can flow fast in some places. They can flow slowly in other places. Rivers can be large or small.

Some rivers flow into a wetland. Some flow into a lake. Some rivers flow into a larger river. Some flow into the ocean.

Compare and Contrast Look at these photos. Tell how they are alike. Tell how they are different.

EXTREME SCIENCE

Wild Rapids

Big Shoals
State Park

The Suwannee River in Big Shoals State Park can flow very fast. It has big rapids. Rapids are fast-moving parts of a river. The rapids here are the fastest in Florida.

The Suwannee River flows through an area with limestone rocks. Some of these rocks fell into the river. The water tumbles over these rocks to make the rapids.

Draw Conclusions Tell what makes water move fast.

Lesson 3

Changes to Land

SC.1.E.5.3 Investigate how magnifiers make things appear bigger and help people see things they could not see without them. SC.1.E.6.3 Recognize that some things in the world around us happen fast and some happen slowly. (Also SC.1.N.1.1, SC.1.N.1.3, and LAFS.K12.R1.1)

Vocabulary

weathering

erosion

landslide

lava

wildfire

I **can** describe some fast and slow ways Earth changes.

Jumpstart Discovery!

Gentle waves splash on the sand. Act it out.

Big waves crash against the sand and rocks. Act it out.

uInvestigate Lab

How can water help change rock?

Geologists study how Earth's surface changes. They observe land and water. How do you think the land changes over time?

Materials
- 2 pieces of sandstone
- 1 jar with a lid
- water
- hand lens

Procedure

☐ 1. Observe the rocks. Notice their size and shape. **Draw** your observations.

☐ 2. How can water change rock? Use the water and jar. Draw your observations.

Science Practice

You **record** or draw observations during an investigation to show what happened.

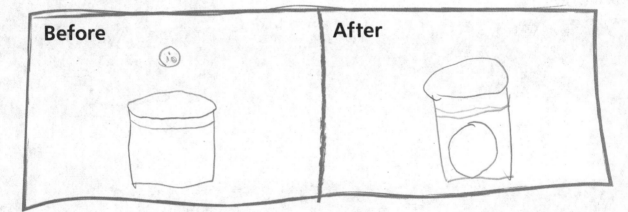

Before	After

Analyze and Interpret Data

3. **Tell** Explain what happened to the rocks.

INTERACTIVITY

Go online to learn more about how Earth's surface changes.

Slow Changes

Earth's surface is always changing. Some changes happen slowly.

Weathering happens when rocks break apart. Water and temperature changes cause weathering. After rocks break apart, wind and water can remove small pieces from rocks. This is called **erosion**. Weathering and erosion slowly change the shape of land.

Visual Literacy Look at the pictures. These photos show different landforms along the river. Tell about each photo. Use vocabulary.

Quest Connection

Tell how fast moving water can change the land in the Grand Canyon.

Fast Changes

Heavy rain can cause a flood. It can make rivers rise and overflow onto the land. Water can rush down a hill. It pushes soil and rocks down. This is a **landslide**.

The rock deep inside Earth is very hot. When a volcano erupts, melted rock rises to the surface. It pours out of the volcano as **lava**.

Lightning strikes! The sudden heat can set a tree on fire. Wind blows the flames to other trees. Then a large fire, known as a **wildfire**, burns through the forest.

☑️ **Reading Check** Draw Conclusions Underline words that show how floods change Earth's surface.

flood

volcano

wildfire

landslide

What are *fast* and **slow** changes?

Hills with steep slopes sometimes have landslides when heavy rains fall. How does the land change after a landslide?

Materials

- wooden board
- large plastic container
- small plastic containers
- water
- sand
- dirt
- pebbles

Procedure

☐ 1. Think of a way to use these materials to make your own landslide.

☐ 2. Make a plan. Show it to your teacher.

☐ 3. Make your landslide. **Collect data.**

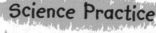

Science Practice

You **collect data** to gather information.

Observations

Drawing of hillside

Observations after water added

Analyze and Interpret Data

4. Tell Explain how the landslide changed the land. Use your data.

🖱 **INTERACTIVITY**

Go online to learn more about Earth's surface.

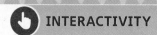

Mystery
Along the River

What clues show how Earth's surface changes?

Read through the pages. Find the photos I took of the plants along the river. Find photos of fast and slow moving water. Look at how the land changed along the river. Why did I see all of these different things?

Show What You Found

Now make a scrapbook. Draw pictures of the photos I took. Write new captions that explain why there are different types of plants and animals at different places along the river.

QUEST CHECK ✓ OFF

Geologist

Geologists are scientists. They study the land and water on places all over Earth. Some geologists study what Earth was like long, long ago. Other geologists study rock formations to tell us how they formed. Some geologists study volcanoes while others study glaciers! Geology is a fun career.

What would you like to ask a geologist?

_____

_____

_____

_____

_____

_____

The Essential Question

What can you tell about Earth's surface?

Show What You Learned

Tell a partner what you learned about Earth's surface and its changes.

Read each question and choose or write the best answer.

1. What nonliving things do you see in the photo?
   a. water, rocks, soil
   b. plants, soil, rocks
   c. animals, soil, rocks
   d. water, trees, plants

2. An earthworm lives in soil.
Why do worms live in soil, not rock?

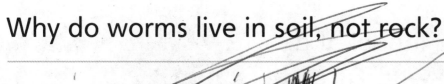

in possibl to
break

3. Which changes happen fast? Which happen
slow? Use the word bank to fill in this table.

weathering	landslide	flood	erosion

Fast Changes	Slow Changes

4. An experiment shows that erosion happens
slower on land with lots of trees. Why?

Read the scenario and answer questions 1–2.

Pablo drew a model of a change on Earth's surface.

1 Which type of change do you observe in the model?

Ⓐ weathering

Ⓑ fast

Ⓒ erosion

Ⓓ slow

idk

2 How can Pablo slow down the changes shown in his model?

Ⓕ He can include air in the environment.

Ⓖ He can include buildings in the environment.

Ⓗ He can include cars in the environment.

Ⓘ He can include water in the environment.

idk

Read the scenario and answer question 3.

Sandra drew a pie graph that shows how much water covers the surface of Earth.

3 How much of Earth's surface is covered by water?

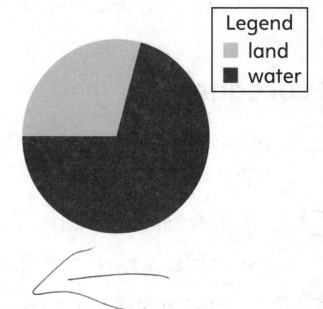

Legend
▨ land
■ water

A almost one-third

B almost one-half

C almost four-fifths

D almost three-fourths

4 How can Hailey model a slow change that shapes Earth's surface?

F She can model waves breaking off small pieces of rock.

G She can model lava flowing from a volcano.

H She can model heavy rain flooding a street.

I She can model a wildfire burning a forest.

How is healthy soil important to plants?

Not all soil is alike. What is the difference between healthy soil and unhealthy soil?

Procedure

☐ 1. Observe the soil and the gravel. Tell what you see.

☐ 2. Plan a way to find out which sample is best for growing seeds.

☐ 3. Water both cups of seeds each day.

☐ 4. Record your observations in "Day 1."

☐ 5. Predict how both seeds will grow.

☐ 6. Observe the cups every few days. Record the changes you see.

Materials

- 2 cups
- gravel
- soil
- seeds
- hand lens
- water
- graduated cylinder

Science Practice

When you **make an explanation**, you tell how and why something happens.

Observations

	Day 1	Day 5	Day 10
Soil without rocks			
Soil with rocks			

Analyze and Interpret Data

7. **Tell** why one group of seeds grew faster than the other.

8. **Draw Conclusions** What do plants need to grow?

_____

_____

Matter and Movement

SC.1.P.8.1 Sort objects by observable properties, such as size, shape, color, temperature (hot or cold), weight (heavy or light), texture, and whether objects sink or float. **SC.1.P.12.1** Demonstrate and describe the various ways that objects can move, such as in a straight line, zigzag, back-and-forth, round-and-round, fast, and slow. **SC.1.P.13.1** Demonstrate that the way to change the motion of an object is by applying a push or a pull. (Also **SC.1.N.1.1, SC.1.N.1.2, SC.1.N.1.3, SC.1.N.1.4, LAFS.1.RI.1.1, LAFS.1.RI.1.3, LAFS.1.RI.4.10, MAFS.K12.MP.2.1, MAFS.K12.MP.5.1, MAFS.1.MD.1.1, MAFS.1.MD.1.a.a,** and **MAFS.1.MD.1.a.b**)

Go online to access
your digital course.

- ▶ VIDEO
- 📖 eTEXT
- 👆 INTERACTIVITY
- ▶ SCIENCE SONG
- 🎮 GAME
- ☑ ASSESSMENT

The Essential Question

How can you describe objects and how they move?

Show What You Know

Look at the photo. Describe how the amusement park ride moves.

STEM Help Deliver Supplies

What affects how objects move?

Hi! My name is Mr. Jackson. I am a mechanical engineer. I design machines and tools. I build and test them.

A catapult is a machine. It sends things from one place to another. I need your help. I need to build a catapult. It is for a rescue mission. It will deliver supplies from a boat. The supplies will go to people on land. You will build a model catapult. The path shows the Quest activities you will complete as you work through the topic. Check off your progress each time you complete an activity with a **QUEST CHECK ✓ OFF** .

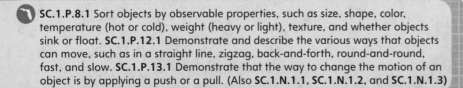

SC.1.P.8.1 Sort objects by observable properties, such as size, shape, color, temperature (hot or cold), weight (heavy or light), texture, and whether objects sink or float. **SC.1.P.12.1** Demonstrate and describe the various ways that objects can move, such as in a straight line, zigzag, back-and-forth, round-and-round, fast, and slow. **SC.1.P.13.1** Demonstrate that the way to change the motion of an object is by applying a push or a pull. (Also **SC.1.N.1.1, SC.1.N.1.2,** and **SC.1.N.1.3**)

 VIDEO
Watch a video about a mechanical engineer.

Quest Check-In 2

Lesson 2
Choose materials for a catapult that would best move supplies.

Quest Check-In Lab 3

Lesson 3 ◆
Use what you have learned about pushes and pulls. Design and build a model catapult!

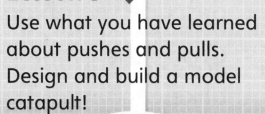

Quest Check-In 1

Lesson 1 ■
Describe objects. Record your observations. Tell how the objects would move when launched by a catapult.

Quest Findings

Complete the Quest! Identify what affects the motion of an object. Explain how a catapult uses pushes and pulls.

How can objects be described?

Scientists observe objects carefully. They pick objects to use based on grouping objects that are alike. How can you sort objects?

Procedure

☐ 1. **Observe** the objects.

☐ 2. Use your own words to describe the objects.

☐ 3. Group the objects that are alike.

Analyze and Interpret Data

4. Compare your observations with others. How are your groups of objects alike? How are they different?

Suggested Materials

- ball
- book
- canned food
- ruler

Science Practice

You **observe** to describe things.

Cause and Effect

An engineer may build machines. Rockets are machines that go to space. Read about how rockets move.

A cause makes something happen. An effect is the result.

GAME

Practice what you learn with the Mini Games.

Space Launch System

NASA is building a powerful rocket. It will go to Mars and beyond. The rocket will have four engines. Engines burn fuel. The engines push out gases from the burning fuel. The rocket goes up. The rocket will send humans and heavy supplies to space.

☑ **Reading Check** **Cause and Effect** Underline what causes a rocket to go up.

NASA's Space Launch System

Lesson 1

Sort Objects

I can describe matter.
I can sort matter.

Vocabulary

matter

weight

texture

float

sink

temperature

Jumpstart Discovery!

Look at the seashells in the photo.

Make a chart that lists the different colors of shells. Tally the number of shells for each category.

uInvestigate Lab

How can you show how objects **are** different?

Sorting helps scientists learn about how objects are alike and different. Do you collect anything that you sort?

Procedure

☐ **1.** Observe the objects. Touch the objects.

☐ **2.** Think of ways the objects are different. **Collect data.** Draw or write how you sorted the objects.

Suggested Materials

✓ • coins

✓ • blocks

✓ • cards

✓ • small toys

Science Practice

You **collect data** to keep records of an investigation.

Observations

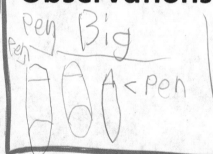

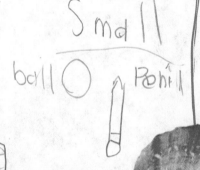

Analyze and Interpret Data

3. Compare your data with another group. What other ways did they sort their objects?

_____

_____

Matter

All objects are made of matter.
Matter is anything that takes up space. A book is made of matter. A pencil is made of matter. You are made of matter, too.

Explain How do you know an object is made of matter?

_____

- - - - - - - - - - - - - - - - - - -

_____

Ways to Describe Matter

Our senses help us make observations. You can describe matter by its shape. A ball is round. You can describe matter by its color. Grass is green. You can describe matter by its size. A truck is big. **Weight** is how heavy something is. The books are heavy. You can describe matter by its **texture**, or how it feels. The end of a paint brush feels soft.

☑ **Reading Check** **Cause and Effect**
Tell what the effect is of letting go of a heavy book.

Quest Connection

Describe the supplies you will launch with your catapult.

More Ways to Describe Objects

Objects can float or sink. Objects that **float** stay on top of a liquid. Lemonade is a liquid. Ice cubes float in the lemonade.

Objects such as coins **sink**, or fall to the bottom of a liquid.

An object can be described by its **temperature,** or how hot or cold something is. The ice in the lemonade is cold.

INTERACTIVITY

Complete an activity on sorting objects.

Literacy ▸ Toolbox

Cause and Effect A marble is placed on top of a liquid. What do you think will be the effect?

LAFS.1.RI.1.3

lemonade

Fly or Flop

What objects would fly through the air if launched by a catapult? How do you know? Observe the objects. Record your observations.

Object	Shape	Size	Weight
cotton ball			
facial tissue			
ball of clay			
flattened clay			

Contrast Tell which objects you think would fly when launched. Tell which objects you think would flop.

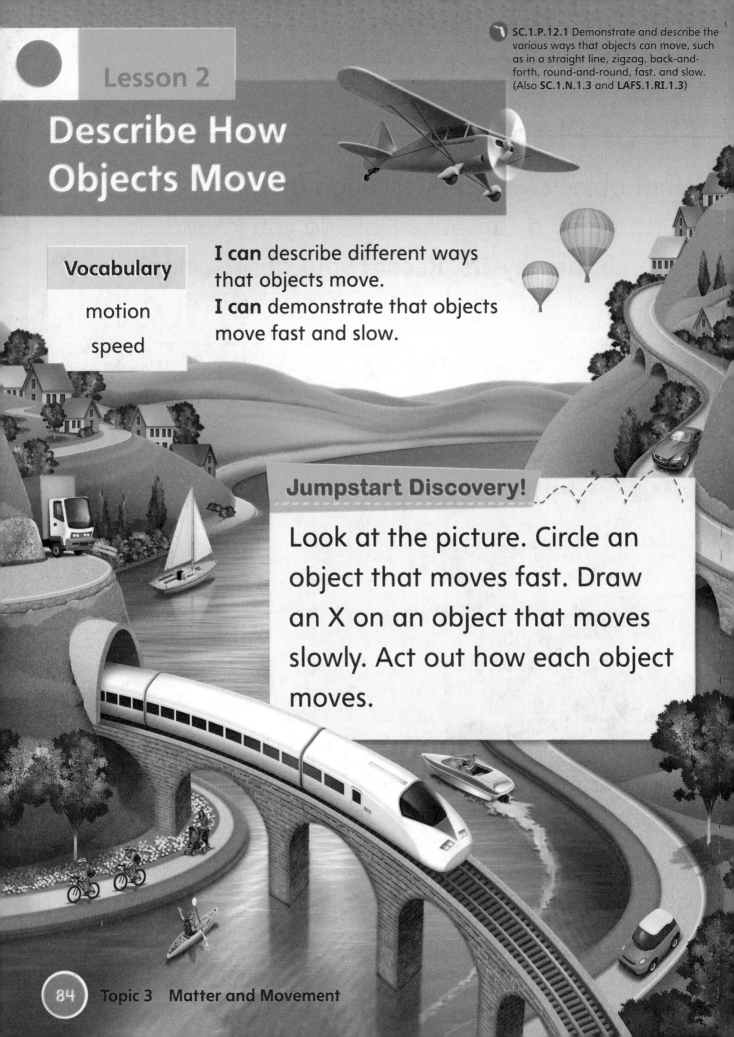

Describe How Objects Move

SC.1.P.12.1 Demonstrate and describe the various ways that objects can move, such as in a straight line, zigzag, back-and-forth, round-and-round, fast, and slow. (Also SC.1.N.1.3 and LAFS.1.RI.1.3)

Vocabulary

motion

speed

I can describe different ways that objects move.
I can demonstrate that objects move fast and slow.

Jumpstart Discovery!

Look at the picture. Circle an object that moves fast. Draw an X on an object that moves slowly. Act out how each object moves.

uInvestigate Lab

What *direction* can objects move in?

Scientists observe how objects move. In what ways can you make these objects move?

Procedure

☐ **1.** Think of how many ways each object can move. Test how each object moves. Observe the direction that each object moves.

☐ **2. Collect data.** Draw each object. Show the direction that each object moved.

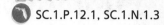

HANDS-ON LAB

SC.1.P.12.1, SC.1.N.1.3

Materials
- spring toy
- wind-up toy
- yo-yo

Science Practice

You **collect data** to learn how things work.

Observations

Analyze and Interpret Data

3. Compare your results with another group. Tell all the ways that the objects can move.

Different Ways to Move

You can describe the motion of an object. **Motion** is how an object moves.

Some objects can move in a straight line. A train can move in a straight line.

Some objects can move back and forth. A swing can move back and forth.

Some objects can move round and round in a circle. Wind can move a pinwheel round and round.

A pinwheel moves round and round in the wind.

A swing moves back and forth.

Other Ways to Move

Some objects can slide. A hockey puck can slide. Some objects move in a zigzag. You move in one direction and then another to zigzag. A person walking across a bridge might zigzag.

Identify Show a zigzag motion. Draw arrows on the photos of the bridge and fence.

Describe Motion

Speed can describe an object. **Speed** is how fast or slow an object moves.

Quest Connection

An object launches from a catapult. How do you think the object will move?

Objects Fly Farther and Faster

Think of materials needed to build a catapult. Supplies go far and fast when the catapult is pulled back more.

Describe Tell which materials you will use to build a catapult.

Describe In what ways will the supplies move?

_____

_____

_____

_____

Infer Look at the catapults. Which will launch the supplies the farthest and fastest? Circle it.

MAFS.K12.MP.2.1, MAFS.1.MD.1.1

Use a Number Line to Compare Movement

A spider can move 2 kilometers in one hour. A cheetah can move 113 kilometers in one hour. A rabbit can move 56 kilometers in one hour. A human can move 24 kilometers in one hour when running.

_____
- - - - - - - - - - - - - - - - - -

cheetah

2 · · · · ◯ · · · · · ◯ · · · · · · · · · 113 · ·

spider

Look at the number line. Label rabbit and human. Write their speeds in the circles.

SC.1.P.8.1, SC.1.P.12.1, SC.1.N.1.1

Design a Boat
That Floats!

INTERACTIVITY

Go online to complete
an activity about
designing a boat.

When you think of a boat, what kind of boat do you imagine? There are tall sailing ships, long canoes, and motor boats. One thing that all boats can do is float.

long canoe

Look at the pictures. What do you observe about how the boats were made? What materials were used? What shapes are they? What ways can these boats move?

sailing ship

226

motor boat

Design It

Boats need to be strong. They must be able to float. They should be able to move quickly. They are usually made from hard, strong materials.

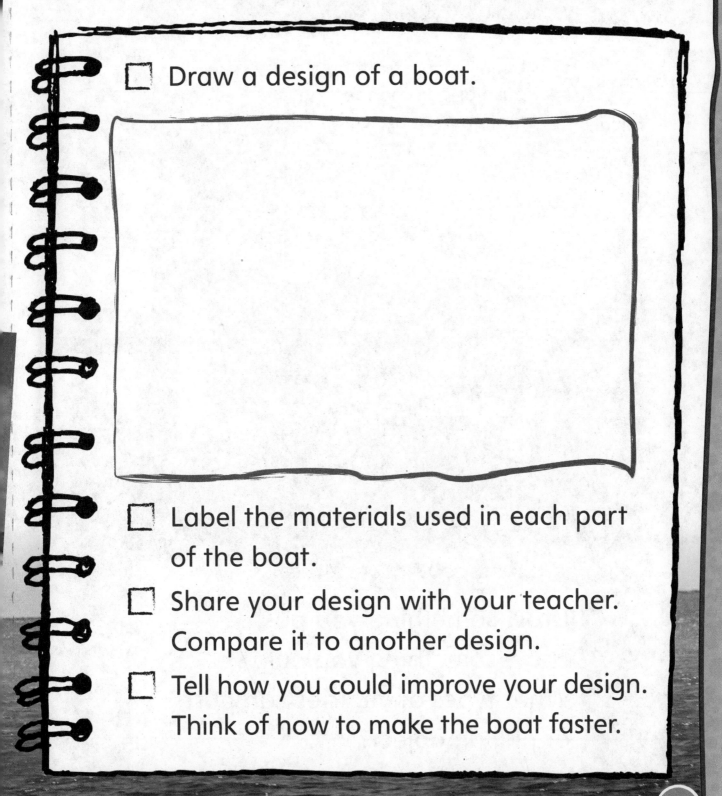

☐ Draw a design of a boat.

☐ Label the materials used in each part of the boat.

☐ Share your design with your teacher. Compare it to another design.

☐ Tell how you could improve your design. Think of how to make the boat faster.

Pushes and Pulls

SC.1.P.13.1 Demonstrate that the way to change the motion of an object is by applying a push or a pull. (Also SC.1.N.1.1, LAFS.1.RI.1.3, MAFS.1.MD.1.a.a, MAFS.1.MD.1.a.b, and MAFS.K12.MP.5.1)

Vocabulary

force

gravity

I can demonstrate how a push or pull changes the motion of an object.

Jumpstart Discovery!

Draw something you push.

Draw something you pull.

What types of vehicles can push or pull an object?

What makes the toy car *move*?

Toy cars cannot start moving on their own.
Something helps make them start moving.
How can you change how the toy car moves?

Materials
- toy car
- string

Procedure

☐ **1.** Plan how you can show how to change the motion of the toy car. Show your plan to your teacher.

☐ **2.** Conduct your investigation.

Science Practice

You **use evidence** to explain why something happens.

Analyze and Interpret Data

3. Tell what made the car move.

4. Use evidence from your investigation. How can you make the car move farther?

_____

_____

_____

_____

_____

Pushes and Pulls

A force moves an object. A **force** is a push or a pull. You pull a car door open to get in. You push a car door closed after you get out.

How do forces on your pencil help you write? You set the pencil tip on paper. You pull the pencil toward you. You push the pencil away from you.

Illustrate Write a capital letter A in the box. Tell when you used a push to write. Tell when you used a pull.

Downward Force

▶ VIDEO

Watch a video about gravity.

When rain falls, it falls to the ground.

When you throw a ball into the air, it returns to the ground.

Gravity is a force that pulls objects to the ground. It causes the rain to fall down. It causes the ball to fall down.

Without gravity, everything on Earth would float away.

☑ **Reading Check** **Cause and Effect**
Circle the effect that gravity has on rain.

Quest Connection

Draw how gravity affects supplies launched from a catapult.

What a Force Can Do

A force can change how objects move.

A force can start to move an object.

A force can stop a moving object.

A force can change the direction of a moving object.

Use more force. The motion of an object changes more. Use less force. The motion of an object changes less.

Visual Literacy

Identify the force in each photo. Circle push or pull.

push

pull

push

pull

push

pull

INTERACTIVITY

Complete an activity on pushes and pulls.

push

pull

push

pull

Lesson 3   Pushes and Pulls   97

How can you design a working catapult model?

Engineers build models to test whether the bigger machine will work. It is time for you to build a model of your catapult. Your model should test the delivery of supplies. How can you use your model to change the motion of an object?

Materials
- safety goggles

Suggested Materials
- plastic spoon
- elastic string
- dowel
- masking tape
- pompom
- clay

Science Practice

You **use a model** to learn about how things work.

⚠ Do not aim your catapult at another student.

⚠ Wear safety goggles.

Design and Build

☐ **1.** Look at the materials. Think about how to make a catapult to test how far an object can travel.

☐ **2.** Draw a design for your **model** catapult. Show your teacher.

☐ **3.** Build the catapult using your design. Run multiple tests to see how you can change the motion of the object.

Observations

Evaluate Your Design

4. Tell how you used a push and pull when testing the catapult.

5. How did you use the catapult to make an object move farther and faster?

INTERACTIVITY

Apply what you learned in the Quest.

Help Deliver Supplies

What affects how objects move?

Think of how to sort objects. Think of how objects move. Think of how to apply pushes and pulls.

Show What You Found

1. Circle things that affect the speed and motion of the supplies when launched.

   weight   color   shape   size

2. Show a push and pull on the catapult photo. Draw arrows. Tell which arrow is for a pull. Tell which arrow is for a push.

3. Tell what will happen if you pull the catapult back more.

QUEST CHECK ✓ OFF

Mechanical Engineer

Mechanical engineers build machines. The machines solve problems. The machines make work easier.

Engineers may build car parts. They may build parts for an airplane. They pick the best materials to use. They design models. They test the model to see how the machine would work. Some engineers use computers to design and test models.

Why is this an important job?

The Essential Question How can you describe objects and how they move?

Show What You Learned
Tell a partner how you can describe the movement of objects.

Read each question and choose or write the best answer.

1. Ben claims that gravity keeps objects in the air. Is Ben correct?

_____

_____

_____

_____

2. Look at the picture of the rubber duck. What do you observe?

   a. It sinks.
   b. It is heavy.
   c. It floats.
   d. It is cold.

3. Which two objects make the same type
   of movement?

   a. a balloon and a ball

   b. a swing and a door

   c. a wheel and a car

   d. a bird and an airplane

4. Look at the pictures. Circle one example
   of a push. Draw an X on a pull.

5. Hilda cleaned up her desk after an
   investigation. Do you think Hilda used
   more "pull" or "push" forces? Explain.

   _____

   _____

   _____

   _____

Read the scenario and answer questions 1–2.

Raul has two objects.

Object A	Object B
large	small
heavy	light
soft	soft
blue	yellow

1 How can Raul sort these objects to show they are alike?

Ⓐ by color

Ⓑ by size

Ⓒ by texture

Ⓓ by weight

2 Raul drops object B, and it falls to the ground. Why does the object fall down?

Ⓕ Gravity moves objects forward.

Ⓖ Gravity pulls objects to the ground.

Ⓗ Gravity moves objects backward.

Ⓘ Gravity pushes objects to the ground.

Read the scenario and answer questions 3–4.

Jennie is investigating what will happen when she adds ice to very cold water in a glass.

3 Predict what will happen to the ice when it is added to the glass of very cold water.

Ⓐ The ice will melt.

Ⓑ The ice will float.

Ⓒ The ice will sink.

Ⓓ The ice will freeze.

4 When Jennie picks up the glass to examine the ice, the glass moves. What type of force is she using to move the glass?

Ⓕ pull

Ⓖ gravity

Ⓗ no force

Ⓘ push

uDemonstrate Lab

What is in the bag?

Engineers need to know how materials look and feel. Using all of our senses helps us learn about objects. How can you identify objects without using sight?

Procedure

☐ 1. Think of a way you can identify different objects without using sight. Choose your materials.

☐ 2. Make a plan for your investigation. Show your plan to your teacher.

☐ 3. **Observe** the objects by using your senses other than sight. Record your data.

Suggested Materials

- paper bag
- eraser
- stress ball
- foil sheet
- bendable straw
- small candle
- toy ring

Science Practice

You **observe** to describe things.

 Do not taste any materials.

Observations

Object	Observations	Identified? Yes or No

Analyze and Interpret Data

4. **Explain** Tell what senses you used.

5. **Identify** What are some ways you can sort objects without looking at them?

_____

_____

6. **Identify** What are some ways you can sort objects only by looking at them?

_____

_____

Living Things

SC.1.L.14.1 Make observations of living things and their environment using the five senses. **SC.1.L.14.2** Identify the major parts of plants, including stem, roots, leaves, and flowers. **SC.1.L.14.3** Differentiate between living and nonliving things. **SC.1.L.17.1** Through observation, recognize that all plants and animals, including humans, need the basic necessities of air, water, food, and space. (Also **SC.1.N.1.1, SC.1.N.1.2, SC.1.N.1.3, SC.1.N.1.4, LAFS.1.RI.1.3 and MAFS.1.MD.1.1**)

Go online to access
your digital course.

▶ VIDEO

📖 eTEXT

👆 INTERACTIVITY

▶ SCIENCE SONG

🎮 GAME

☑ ASSESSMENT

The Essential Question

How do the parts of plants and animals help them?

Show What You Know

Put an **X** on the part of the tortoise that protects it from other animals.

STEM NATURE Copycats

How can you copy plant and animal parts to solve a problem?

Hi! I am Dr. Basha! I am a bioengineer. I make things that help people. I copy plant and animal parts.

Look for ways plants and animals use their parts to live. Use an animal or plant part to help solve a human problem. The path shows the Quest activities you will complete as you work through the topic. Check off your progress each time you complete an activity with a QUEST CHECK ✓ OFF .

SC.1.L.14.1 Make observations of living things and their environment using the five senses. SC.1.L.14.2 Identify the major parts of plants, including stem, roots, leaves, and flowers. SC.1.L.14.3 Differentiate between living and nonliving things. SC.1.L.17.1 Through observation, recognize that all plants and animals, including humans, need the basic necessities of air, water, food, and space.

▶ VIDEO

Watch a video about a bioengineer.

Quest Check-In 3

Lesson 3 ◆

Use what you learned about animal parts. Show how people copy an animal part.

Quest Check-In 4

Lesson 4 ▲

Show how plants and animals use their parts to meet their needs.

Quest Check-In 2

Lesson 2 ●

Use what you learned about plant parts. Show how people copy a plant part.

Quest Check-In Lab 5

Lesson 5 ★

Find out how the color of a snowshoe hare's fur helps it stay alive.

Quest Check-In 1

Lesson 1 ■

Tell which objects are living and which are nonliving. Show how people could copy a part of the living thing.

Quest Findings

Complete the Quest! Copy a plant or animal part. Help solve a human problem.

How can you make a model of a plant?

Scientists use different materials to make models. The models help them study living things. What materials can you use to make a model of a plant?

Design and Build

☐ **1.** Look at the pictures of plants. Choose a plant.

☐ **2.** Choose your materials.

☐ **3.** Design and build your model.

Evaluate Your Model

4. Compare your model to the plant picture. Tell if your model shows all the parts of the plant.

5. Compare your model to models made by other students. Tell how the models are the same and different.

Materials

- pictures of plants

Suggested Materials

- poster board
- construction paper
- crayons
- small objects

Engineering Practice

You **make a model** to help you study the natural world.

Compare and Contrast

LAFS.1.RI.1.3

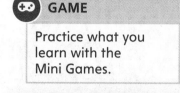

GAME

Practice what you learn with the Mini Games.

You can compare and contrast things. To compare means to see how things are the same. To contrast means to see how things are different.

Geese and Bike Riders

Geese fly in a V shape. The lead goose flies at the tip of the V. That goose flaps its wings. It makes streams of air that rise. The streams help the other geese save energy. A group of bike riders rides single file. The riders who follow the leader save energy.

geese

☑ **Reading Check** Compare and Contrast

Underline how geese and bike riders are the same. Circle how they are different.

bike riders

Nonliving and Living Things

SC.1.L.14.3 Differentiate between living and nonliving things.

SC.1.L.17.1 Through observation, recognize that all plants and animals, including humans, need the basic necessities of air, water, food, and space. (Also SC.1.N.1.1 and LAFS.1.RI.1.3)

I can tell the difference between nonliving things and living things.

Vocabulary

nonliving things

living things

nutrients

Jumpstart Discovery!

Draw a picture of a living thing. Draw a picture of a nonliving thing. Talk about how you can tell if something is living.

How can you tell if something is a living thing?

There are differences between living and nonliving things. How can you observe these differences?

Procedure

☐ 1. **Plan an investigation** to find out which thing is living, the small rocks or the seeds.

☐ 2. Use all the materials.

☐ 3. Show your plan to your teacher. Carry out your plan. Record your observations for 10 days.

Analyze and Interpret Data

4. **Share** what happened to the seeds and the rocks. Which ones are living things? Tell a partner.

Materials

- 2 plastic cups
- measuring cup
- soil
- 2 pinto bean seeds
- 2 small rocks
- water
- graduated cylinder
- tape
- marker

Science Practice

You can **plan an investigation** to answer a question you have about the natural world.

 Wash your hands when done.

Nonliving Things

Nonliving things are things that do not grow or change on their own. Nonliving things do not move on their own. They do not need air or shelter. They do not need food or water. Toys are nonliving things. Rocks are nonliving things.

INTERACTIVITY

Go online to learn more about living and nonliving things.

toys

☑ **Reading Check** **Compare and Contrast** Underline words that describe something that nonliving things cannot do. Tell if they can move on their own.

stream

Living Things

Living things are things that grow and change on their own. Living things need food and water.

Nonliving things do not change on their own. Many living things can move on their own. Animals are living things. A deer is a living thing. Plants are also living things.

Literacy ▸ Toolbox

Compare and Contrast What is one way living things and nonliving things are different?

LAFS.1.RI.1.3

Identify Underline two ways that tell how living things are alike.

deer

Needs of Plants and Animals

All living things have needs. Plants and animals need water and air. They need space to live and grow. People have these needs, too.

Plants need sunlight to make food. Plants use their roots to get water and nutrients from the soil. **Nutrients** are materials that make the bodies of living things work. Plants need sunlight to make food. People and animals get nutrients by eating plants and other animals.

Differentiate Underline how animals get food. Circle how plants get food.

Quest Connection

You use a straw to drink. What part of a plant is like a straw? Tell a partner.

young plants

Living and Nonliving

Living things have parts that help them live.
Nonliving things do not have these parts.

Identify Circle the living things.
Draw an **X** on the nonliving things.

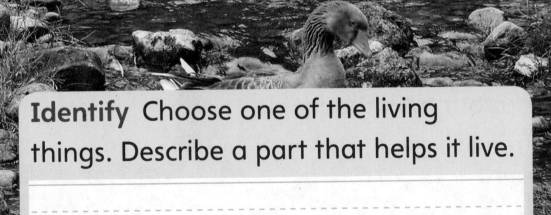

Identify Choose one of the living
things. Describe a part that helps it live.

_____

_____

_____

Plant Parts

▶ VIDEO

Watch a video about roots.

SC.1.L.14.2 Identify the major parts of plants, including stem, roots, leaves, and flowers. SC.1.L.17.1 Through observation, recognize that all plants and animals, including humans, need the basic necessities of air, water, food, and space. (Also SC.1.N.1.3 and LAFS.1.RI.1.3)

Vocabulary

root

stem

leaf

I can identify the major parts of plants.

I can explain how plant parts help plants.

Jumpstart Discovery!

Look at the tree's leaves. Talk about how the leaves help the tree live. Look at the tree's trunk. Talk about how the trunk helps the tree live.

What do the *parts* of a plant look like?

Scientists study plant parts to learn what they do. How can you observe plant parts?

Materials

- a plant
- hand lens
- crayons

Procedure

☐ **1. Observe** the parts of the plant. Use all of the materials. Draw a picture of each part.

Science Practice

You **observe** when you look closely at things.

⚠ **Wash your hands when done.**

Analyze and Interpret Data

2. Explain how you think the shape of the stem helps the plant.

_____

_____

_____

3. Tell about an object that people make that is like a plant stem.

Roots

Plants have parts that help them get what they need to live and grow. Many plants have roots. A **root** is the part of a plant that takes in water.

Roots respond to gravity and moisture and grow into the soil. Roots hold the plant in the ground. Roots grow toward water. Roots get water and nutrients from the soil.

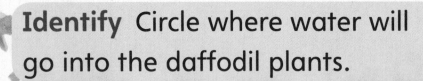

Identify Circle where water will go into the daffodil plants.

Quest Connection

Tell what features of roots people might want to copy. Why would people want to do this?

Stems and Leaves

INTERACTIVITY

Go online to learn more about plant parts.

Many plants have stems and leaves. Leaves and stems respond to the sun by growing toward it.

A **stem** is the part of a plant that takes water from the roots to the leaves and holds the plant up. Water and nutrients move from the roots. They move up the stem and into the leaves.

A **leaf** is the part of a plant that makes food. The leaves use sunlight, water, and nutrients to do this. The spines on a cactus are leaves. They protect the plant.

☑ **Reading Check** Compare and Contrast Draw a line under something a stem does. Draw a circle around something a leaf does.

roots

Flowers and Fruits

Many plants have flowers and fruits. Flowers and fruits help make new plants. Flowers contain eggs and pollen. These are used to make seeds. The fruit holds the seeds of a plant. The fruit keeps the seeds safe. Animals eat fruit. This helps seeds move from place to place.

Literacy ▸ Toolbox

Compare and Contrast Circle words that tell what flowers contain. Underline something fruit does.

LAFS.1.RI.1.3

Predict What are some ways seeds can move from one place to another?

_____

_____

flowers and fruits

desert wildflowers

Roots Help Plants Survive

Some plants have just one thick root called a taproot. It goes deep into the soil and gets water. The taproot helps the plant stay where it is.

Identify Find something in the picture that works like a taproot.

dandelion with taproot

tent stake

Animal Parts

▶ **VIDEO**

Go online to learn how animals use their senses.

SC.1.L.17.1 Through observation, recognize that all plants and animals, including humans, need the basic necessities of air, water, food, and space. (Also **SC.1.N.1.1** and **SC.1.N.1.2**)

Vocabulary

gills

scales

I can identify the major parts of animals.

I can explain how animal parts help animals.

Jumpstart Discovery!

Look at the leopard's eyes. Talk about how seeing helps it. Look at the leopard's paws. Talk about how paws help it move.

How do whiskers help a cat?

Scientists know that animals use their senses. Their senses tell about the environment. How do whiskers help a cat know how big an opening is?

Materials

- boxes or tubes with different-sized openings
- styrofoam ball
- tape
- pipe cleaners

Design and Build

☐ 1. Use the materials. Make a model of the head and whiskers of a cat.

☐ 2. Make a plan. Test how whiskers help a cat get through openings.

☐ 3. Test your model. Record your data.

Engineering Practice

You **use models** to see how something works.

Evaluate Your Design

4. Compare your observations with the observations from another group. Tell how the shape of the whiskers helps them give information to the cat.

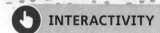

INTERACTIVITY

Go online to learn more about animal parts.

How Animals Move

Animals have different body parts. Some body parts help animals move. Animals move to find food and water.

Many animals, like bears, have legs. Fish have fins. Horses and other animals have hooves. Birds have wings.

black bear

Explain Underline words that tell what animals use to move.

Connecting Concepts ▸ Toolbox

Structure and Function The shape of an animal's body parts give clues to how the animal moves. Look at the feet on the black bear. How do the feet help the bear move? Describe one way a bear might use its claws. 🌀 SC.1.N.1.1, CCC.6

Body Coverings and Ways of Breathing

Animals' body coverings protect them. Hair or fur grows from the skin of many animals. Feathers grow from the skin of birds. Fish and snakes have hard plates called **scales**. Many ocean animals and insects have hard shells.

People and many animals have lungs. They draw in air through their noses. **Gills** are parts on fish that let them breathe underwater.

Identify Underline words that tell the names of different body coverings.

feathers on a bird

scales on a snake

gills on a fish

Animals' Senses and Responses

Animals use their eyes to see. They use their ears to hear. A meerkat uses its ears to listen for danger. Animals smell things and taste things. They touch things with their bodies.

Animals' senses give them information about the world. The information helps them grow and live. Some information tells them they are in danger. Animals use their senses to stay safe.

meerkat

Quest Connection

Animal eyes often see farther than human eyes. Tell a partner a tool people made to see farther.

Different Shapes, Different Uses

Different birds have different beaks.
Some beaks have sharp points.
Some beaks are shaped like hooks.

Differentiate Which beak is the right shape for making holes in trees? Circle it.

woodpecker

eagle

Analyze People make tools based on animal parts. Tell something people do with a pointed tool.

SC.1.L.17.1 SC.1.N.1.3

▶ **VIDEO**

Watch a video about how bioengineers solve problems.

Design a Tool

Bioengineers study plant and animal parts. They might study a turtle shell to design a better bicycle helmet.

Would you like to help a bioengineer solve a problem?

tortoise

Design It

Animals use tools. Look at the photos. Design a tool you can use to solve a problem.

chimpanzee

☐ Choose an animal tool you will copy. Think about the tool you will make. What do you think people could use this tool for?

crow

_____
_____
_____
_____
_____
_____

☐ Think of what you need to build the tool.

☐ Design the tool.

☐ Describe how your tool will work. How can you make it better?

_____
_____
_____
_____

People Learn from Plant and Animal Parts

VIDEO

Watch a video about biomimicry.

SC.1.L.14.2 Identify the major parts of plants, including stem, roots, leaves, and flowers. SC.1.L.17.1 Through observation, recognize that all plants and animals, including humans, need the basic necessities of air, water, food, and space. (Also SC.1.N.1.1 and MAFS.1.MD.1.1)

Vocabulary

mimic

I can demonstrate how people can learn from plant and animal parts.

Jumpstart Discovery!

Be a leaf. Act it out. Tell how a leaf helps a plant live. Be a squirrel. Act it out. Tell how a squirrel's legs help it live.

What can people learn from an acorn shell?

Acorns fall from oak trees. How does the hard shell help the acorn?

Materials
- acorn
- hand lens
- small hammer

Procedure

☐ **1.** Use all the materials. Make a plan to break the shell of the acorn. Show your plan to your teacher.

☐ **2.** Conduct your investigation. Record your observations.

Science Practice

You **explain** when you tell how something works.

⚠ **Wear goggles if you are using a hammer.**

Analyze and Interpret Data

3. Explain how the hard shell helps the acorn.

_____

_____

4. How can people copy what the acorn does to help people stay alive?

_____

_____

People Mimic Nature

Plants and animals have different body parts. People look at how plants function. They look at how animals solve problems. People get ideas from other living things. People **mimic**, or copy, what plants and animals do. They do this to get what they need to live.

Quest Connection

Tell why people can get good ideas about solving problems from plants and animals.

barbed wire fence

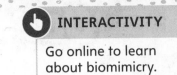
INTERACTIVITY

Go online to learn about biomimicry.

Porcupines have sharp quills. Animals come near them. They raise their quills. Their quills keep animals from eating them. People mimicked how nature uses sharp things. People made fences with many sharp metal points. Farmers put their cows and sheep inside the fences. The fences keep animals from walking away.

porcupine

Predict Do you think people will ever stop getting ideas from other living things? Tell why or why not.

☑ Reading Check **Compare and Contrast** Underline words that show how porcupines use their quills to protect themselves.

A Sticky Invention

Burrs are plant seeds that stick to things.

burr

An inventor studied how burrs stick. He invented a fastener. One side has hooks like burrs. The other side has loops like fabric. The two sides stick together. People use hook-and-loop fasteners in products that help people. One product is a splint. It wraps around an arm, leg, hand, or foot. It holds broken bones or pulled muscles in place.

splint

Identify What is another way that people use hook-and-loop fasteners?

 MAFS.1.MD.1.1

Order Objects by Length

Many kinds of plants have the same parts. The parts are different sizes. Trees have trunks. The trunks are different lengths.

Compare Look at the pictures. Order the trunks by their lengths. Label the longest trunk with a 1. Label the shortest trunk with a 3.

Where Plants and Animals Live

▶ **VIDEO**

Watch a video about land and water environments.

SC.1.L.14.1 Make observations of living things and their environment using the five senses. (Also SC.1.N.1.1 and SC.1.N.1.4)

Vocabulary

environment

I can use my senses to observe living things in their environments.

Jumpstart Discovery!

Draw a picture of a plant or animal. Talk about what the plant or animal needs to live. Talk about how it gets what it needs from where it lives.

HANDS-ON LAB

 SC.1.L.14.1, SC.1.N.1.4

What happens to a water plant out of water?

If you take a plant from where it lives, can it survive? Could a wetland plant live in a desert?

Materials

- wax paper
- string
- paper clips
- container with water
- scissors

Procedure

☐ **1.** Use the materials to build a model of a plant that lives in water.

☐ **2.** Make a plan to investigate what would happen if the water plant was on land.

☐ **3.** Record your observations.

⚠ **Be careful using scissors.**

Science Practice

You **observe** things in nature to ask and answer questions about them.

Analyze and Interpret Data

4. Evaluate What happened to your model water plant when it was on land? Tell a partner why.

5. Draw Conclusions Can the water plant live on land? Tell a partner.

Environments

Plants and animals live in environments. This is a lake environment. An **environment** is everything that is around a living thing. Nonliving things like water and air are part of environments. Living things like plants and animals are part of environments. People are part of environments, too. Living things get what they need in their environment.

Science Practice
▸Toolbox
Ask Questions Ask questions about environments.
SC.1.N.1.1

Explain Underline nonliving things that are part of environments. Circle living things that are part of environments.

lake environment

Sensing Environments

You can use your senses to learn about environments. You can see things in an environment. You can hear things in an environment. You can touch things in an environment. You can smell things in an environment. You can use your senses to learn about this forest environment.

forest environment

Identify Circle words that tell how you use your senses.

Quest Connection

Tell how people use their senses to learn about environments. Tell how this helps them mimic nature.

Land and Water Environments

There are land and water environments. Living things get what they need in them. You can use your senses to learn about them.

The ocean is salt water. The water is very deep. Fish live there. Seaweed lives there.

☑ **Reading Check** **Compare and Contrast** Tell how a wetland is like an ocean. Tell how a wetland is different from an ocean.

Visual Literacy Look at the picture of a meadow. Write how the mouse is getting what it needs to live.

It is very dry in a desert. The ground is sand or hard soil. Few plants and animals live there.

Many grasses live in a meadow. There are few trees. Birds and other small animals live there.

INTERACTIVITY

Go online to explore different environments.

Water covers the soil in a wetland. The water is not very deep. Birds and grasses live there.

Quest Check-In — Lab

How do snowshoe hares stay safe?

People and animals use color to stay safe. Snowshoe hares have fur that is brown in the summer and white in the winter. Can you think of ways people use color when they are outside?

Materials

• Landscape and Hares sheet
• crayons

Science Practice

You use a model to answer questions about nature.

Procedure

☐ **1.** Look at the pictures of the snowshoe hares.

☐ **2.** Use the Landscape and Hares sheet to learn how the fur color of the hares keeps them safe.

☐ **3.** Record your notes in the chart.

Picture	How Color Affects the Animal or Environment
summer	
winter	
hares	

Analyze and Interpret Data

4. **Predict** What color is the fur on the hare likely to be in winter?

_____

_____

5. **Draw Conclusions** What might people learn from how animals use color? Tell a partner.

⬇ **INTERACTIVITY**

Apply what you learned in the Quest.

NATURE Copycats

How can you copy plant and animal parts to solve a problem?

Think about what you have learned about plant and animal parts. What can people learn from plants and animals?

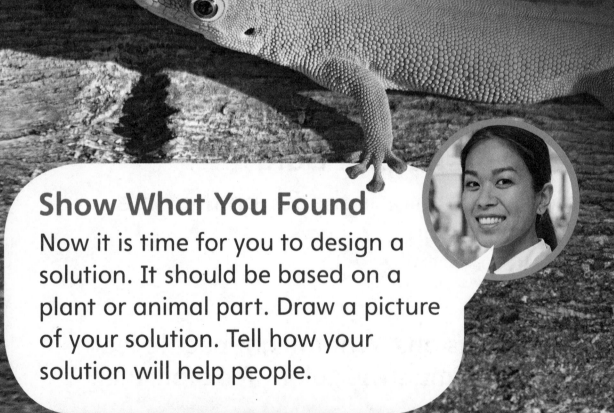

Show What You Found

Now it is time for you to design a solution. It should be based on a plant or animal part. Draw a picture of your solution. Tell how your solution will help people.

QUEST CHECK ✓ **OFF**

Bioengineer

Bioengineers study plants and animals. They use what they learn to build things. Bioengineers make things that help sick or hurt people. They make artificial arms and legs. They try to solve other problems, too.

Some bioengineers work at colleges. Some work in hospitals. Some work for companies.

What problem would you try to solve if you were a bioengineer?

_____

_____

_____

_____

The Essential Question

How do the parts of plants and animals help them?

Show What You Learned

Tell a partner what you learned about how the parts of plants and animals help them live.

Read each question and choose or write the best answer.

1. How are all living things alike?
   a. They all need food.
   b. They all need help to move.
   c. They all have the same parts.
   d. They all live in the same environment.

2. Look at the picture of the plant. Label the plant's parts. Use the word bank.

   | roots   stem   leaves   flowers   fruit |

3. Bart wants to mimic the eyes of a cat. He researched two different types of human technology.

Telescope	Night-vision glasses
helps to magnify objects	helps to see objects in the dark

Which human technology do you think will best meet Bart's needs? Explain.

_____

_____

_____

_____

4. Look at your answer to question 3. Describe how people could use what they learned from studying cats. Describe a design that people could make to solve a human problem.

_____

_____

_____

_____

Read the scenario and answer questions 1–2.

Christie recorded living and nonliving things she observed in her backyard.

Living things	Nonliving things
trees	bench
flowers	hose
squirrel	flower pot
rock	water
bird	air

1 Christie made a mistake on her chart. Why are Christie's observations incorrect?

Ⓐ A flower is not a living thing.

Ⓑ Water is not a living thing.

Ⓒ A rock is not a living thing.

Ⓓ A bench is not a living thing.

2 Christie observed a rock. How could she tell that the rock was hard?

Ⓕ She used her sense of sight.

Ⓖ She used her sense of smell.

Ⓗ She used her sense of hearing.

Ⓘ She used her sense of touch.

Read the scenario and answer questions 3–4.

Charlie compared the major parts of a plant.

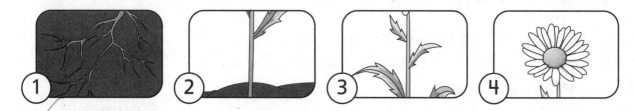

3 Charlie claims that diagram 2 shows the stem. Which statement **best** supports his claim?

Ⓐ The stem holds the seeds of the plant.

Ⓑ The stem moves water and nutrients to different parts of the plant.

Ⓒ The stem uses sunlight, water, and nutrients to make food.

Ⓓ The stem gets water and nutrients from the soil.

4 How do you know that plants are living things?

Ⓕ Plants need food and water to survive.

Ⓖ Plants need rocky soil to survive.

Ⓗ Plants need animals to survive.

Ⓘ Plants need large environments to survive.

How do the spines of cacti help them?

Cactus plants have spines. Spines are very sharp leaves. How can you use a model to test how spines help cacti?

Design and Build

☐ **1.** Study the picture of the cactus spines.

☐ **2.** Choose your materials to make a model.

☐ **3.** Design and build your model.

☐ **4.** Try to touch the stem without touching the spines. Try three times. Write what happens in the table.

Materials

- scissors
- crayons
- tape
- glue

Suggested Materials

- different types of paper
- variety of cardboard objects
- variety of long, thin objects

Engineering Practice

You **make a model** to help you study nature.

 Be careful using scissors and other objects with sharp points.

Observations

Trial Number	Observations
1	
2	
3	

Evaluate Your Model

4. Identify Show a partner the spines and stem on your model.

5. Explain Tell what would happen to an animal that tried to eat the cactus.

6. Use Evidence Tell how the spines help the cactus.

Parents and Offspring

SC.1.L.16.1 Make observations that plants and animals closely resemble their parents, but variations exist among individuals within a population. **SC.1.L.17.1** Through observation, recognize that all plants and animals, including humans, need the basic necessities of air, water, food, and space. (Also **SC.1.N.1.3**, **SC.1.N.1.4**, **SC.K2.CS-CP.2.4**, **LAFS.1.RI.1.2**, and **MAFS.1.MD.1.1**, **MAFS.1.NBT.2.3**)

Go online to access your digital course.

▶ VIDEO

📖 eTEXT

👆 INTERACTIVITY

▶ SCIENCE SONG

🎮 GAME

☑ ASSESSMENT

The Essential Question How are parents and their young alike and different?

Show What You Know

Circle the parent. Put an X on the young.

Find the Parents

What clues help us find a young animal's parent?

Hi! I'm Ms. Swift! I'm a nature scientist. I help keep plants and animals safe. I need your help.

Someone left a gate open at the zoo! Many animals escaped. Help me find the missing parents of these three young animals. Look for clues as you read. The path shows the Quest activities you will complete as you work through the topic. Check off your progress each time you complete an activity with a **QUEST CHECK ✔ OFF** .

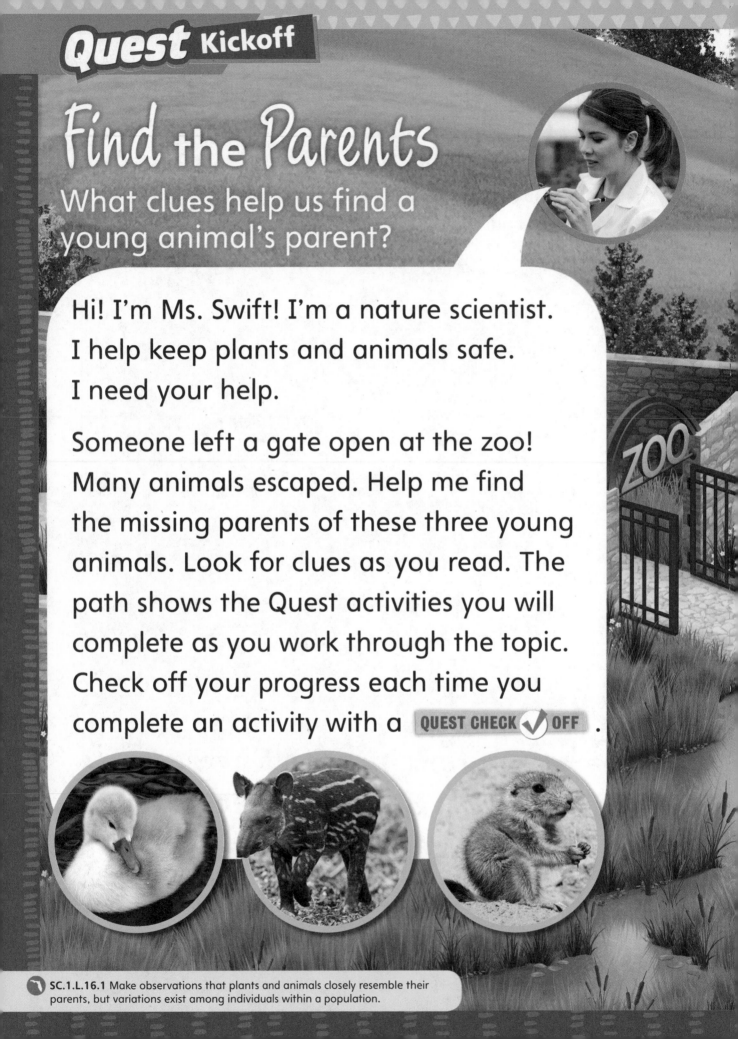

SC.1.L.16.1 Make observations that plants and animals closely resemble their parents, but variations exist among individuals within a population.

▶ VIDEO

Watch a video about a nature scientist.

Quest Check-In 2

Lesson 2 ●

Use what you learned about parents and young to match the puppies to their parents.

Quest Check-In 3

Lesson 3 ◆

Read more about animal behaviors and how bear parents help their cubs.

Quest Check-In Lab 1

Lesson 1 ■

Use what you learned about animal life cycles to tell how two animal life cycles are alike and different.

Quest Findings

Complete the Quest! Find a fun way to show how the young animals and their parents are alike and different.

Which mouse is longer?

Nature scientists make observations of living things to answer questions. What observation can you make to answer the question in the title?

Science Practice

You **make observations** to help answer scientific questions.

Procedure

☐ **1.** Think of a way you can make observations to find out which mouse is longer.

☐ **2.** Collect and record your data.

Mice shown are actual size.

Analyze and Interpret Data

3. Look at your data. Circle data that show which mouse is longer.

4. Tell how the mice are different.

Main Idea and Details

LAFS.1.RI.1.2

GAME

Practice what you learn with the Mini Games.

Nature scientists observe animals. Read about the main idea and details of geese and their young.

The main idea is what the sentences are about. Details tell about the main idea.

Geese and Their Young

Geese keep their young safe. They build nests for the young. The young sleep near their parents. Geese and their young find grass to eat. Parents stay near while young eat.

☑ **Reading Check** **Main Idea and Details**
Circle the main idea. Underline two details.

geese and their goslings

Plant and Animal Life Cycles

VIDEO

Watch a video about life cycles.

SC.1.L.16.1 Make observations that plants and animals closely resemble their parents, but variations exist among individuals within a population. (Also **SC.1.N.1.4** and **LAFS.1.RI.1.2**)

Vocabulary

life cycle

offspring

I can observe the life cycles of some plants and animals.

Jumpstart Discovery!

Circle a tomato, red pepper, and cucumber in the picture. What do you think is inside each of these?

uInvestigate Lab

How do plants grow and change?

Nature scientists ask questions about plants. How do you know a plant grows and changes?

Materials

- seeds (lima beans, radish, or sunflower)
- wet paper towel
- resealable plastic bag
- hand lens

Procedure

☐ **1.** Choose one kind of seed.

☐ **2.** Use all of the other materials. Make a plan to see how seeds grow. Tell your teacher your plan before you start.

Science Practice

You **make observations** to help answer a question.

☐ **3. Observe** your seeds every other day for ten days. Draw what you observe.

Analyze and Interpret Data

4. Tell how the seeds changed.

Life Cycle of a Plant

A **life cycle** is the stages a living thing goes through during its life. A watermelon plant begins as a seed. Then it grows into a small plant. The plant changes. It grows into an adult plant.

Draw the missing arrow in the life cycle.

Literacy ▸ Toolbox

Main Idea and Details
All living things grow and change is the main idea. Use the details to tell how a watermelon plant changes during its life cycle. LAFS.1.RI.1.2

fruit with seeds

adult plant   young plant

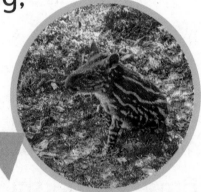

INTERACTIVITY

Compare the life cycles of a chicken and a tapir.

Life Cycle of an Animal

Animals have life cycles, too. A tapir is an animal that lives in the forest. A young tapir will grow and change. It will look like its parents.

It will have **offspring**, or young, of its own.

☑ Reading Check

Main Idea and Details Circle the main idea. Underline two details.

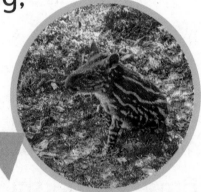

newborn tapir

young tapir

adult tapir

Quest Connection

Tell how the newborn tapir grows and changes.

How are the life cycles alike and different?

You have learned about the life cycle of a plant and an animal. Now find out how the life cycles of two animals are alike and different.

Procedure

☐ 1. Choose two animals from the worksheet. Cut out each part of the two life cycles.

☐ 2. Arrange the cycles in the two boxes. Paste them in each box.

☐ 3. What can you add to each to make it a cycle? Add it.

☐ 4. **Observe** how each animal grows and changes.

Materials
- Animal Life Cycles worksheet
- scissors
- glue stick

Science Practice

You **compare observations** to learn about patterns in nature.

⚠️ **Be careful when using scissors.**

Analyze and Interpret Data

5. **Describe** the life cycle of each animal.

6. **What** patterns do you see?

Observe Parents and Young

SC.1.L.16.1 Make observations that plants and animals closely resemble their parents, but variations exist among individuals within a population. (Also SC.1.N.1.3 and MAFS.1.MD.1.1)

Vocabulary

compare

contrast

I can understand that young plants and animals are like, but not exactly like, their parents.

Jumpstart Discovery!

Be a young plant. Act it out.

Be a parent plant. Act it out.

Talk about the two plants.

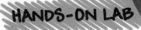

What do young plants look like?

Nature scientists can observe young plants. They make sure they are healthy like the parent plants.

Materials
- paper
- crayons

Science Practice

You **observe** when you look closely at things.

Procedure

☐ **1.** Look at the two parent plants.

☐ **2.** Choose one of the parent plants. Draw it on a piece of paper.

☐ **3.** What do you think the young plant of this parent would look like? Draw it.

Analyze and Interpret Data

4. Observe the young plants of the other groups. Tell what you notice.

Alike and Different

Young plants and animals look like their parents in some ways. They look different in other ways.

Compare these two animals. To **compare** is to tell how two things are alike. Contrast the two animals. To **contrast** is to tell how two things are different.

orangutans

Plants Are Alike

▶ VIDEO
Watch a video about parents and their young.

Plants of the same kind are alike. All marigold plants have colorful flowers.

A young plant and a parent plant are alike. They both have stems and leaves.

Look at these plants. The leaves on both plants look alike. They are the same shape.

Compare Circle the parts of the plants that are alike.

young marigold plant

parent marigold plant

Plants Are Different

Plants of the same kind are different. Hyacinth flowers can have different colors.

hyacinths

A young plant and a parent plant are different. The plants are different sizes.

Parent plants have more leaves. Parent plants often have more flowers.

☑ Reading Check **Main Idea and Details**
Underline a detail about parents.

Draw a young plant and its parent.

Animals Are Alike

Animals of the same kind are alike.
All prairie dogs have fur.

Young animals and their parents are alike.
Prairie dogs have the same body parts.
Their faces are the same shape.

INTERACTIVITY

Compare how living things and their parents are alike and different.

> **Compare** Circle two ways parents and young are alike.

Quest Connection

Tell what clues will help you find the missing parents.

prairie dogs

Animals Are Different

Animals of the same kind are different. Rabbits can be brown, black, or white.

Young animals and their parents are different, too. Young rabbits are smaller than their parents.

Contrast Draw an **X** on a rabbit that is different from the others.

Math ▸ Toolbox

Compare Numbers
You can compare how long objects are. Parent rabbits have longer ears than young rabbits. Use cubes to measure the lengths of two classroom objects. Which is longer?

MAFS.1.MD.1.1

rabbits

Alike and Different

Puppies may look like their parents.
Puppies may look different, too.

Airedale

St. Bernard

Identify Match the puppies to their parents.

Contrast Tell how the puppies look different from one another.

иEngineer It! Design STEM

INTERACTIVITY

Go online to learn about code for computers.

Code the Way!

Game code turns the player's movements into actions in the game.

Would you like to write code for video games?

Learn about a career as a software engineer.

gamers

Design It

Video games use codes to make the characters move. Build a code for a video game. Help the robot owl reach the young owlets.

☐ Use a coin to represent a robot owl.

☐ Place the coin in the top left square.

☐ Use the **symbol key** to write code. Guide the robot owl through the maze.

symbol key

▶	▲
Move right 1 space	Move up 1 space
◀	▼
Move left 1 space	Move down 1 space

Your Code

1.	2.	3.	4.	5.	6.
7.	8.	9.	10.	11.	12.

SC.1.L.17.1 Through observation, recognize that all plants and animals, including humans, need the basic necessities of air, water, food, and space. (Also SC.1.N.1.3 and MAFS.1.NBT.2.3)

Lesson 3

Patterns in Animal Behavior

Vocabulary

protect

pattern

behavior

I can tell what animals need.
I can explain how the behaviors of parents and their young help the young survive.

Jumpstart Discovery!

Think of an animal home.

Draw it on a sheet of paper.

How did it help the young animals?

Tell a partner what you know.

HANDS-ON LAB

SC.1.L.17.1, SC.1.N.1.3

How do nests protect eggs?

Parent birds build nests. Nests protect the eggs.

Design and Build

☐ **1.** Circle the materials you will use to build your nest.

☐ **2.** Design your nest. Build it.

☐ **3.** Place marbles in your nest.

Evaluate Your Design

4. Tell how your nest helps protect the marbles.

5. How is your nest like a bird's nest?

Materials

- 1-inch marbles
- nest materials (paper, newspaper, leaves, small paper bags, grass, twigs, modeling clay)

Engineering Practice

You **plan a design** before you build something.

 Wash your hands when you are done.

Animal Needs

An animal needs food. An animal needs water. An animal needs shelter.

wood mouse

Identify Circle a photo that shows shelter.

Underline a photo that shows food.

red fox

bears

Parents Help Young

▶ **VIDEO**

Watch a video about animal behavior.

lions

woodpeckers

Parents feed their young.
They help young find water.

Identify Circle the parent in each photo.

Quest Connection

Tell why young animals need their parents.

Parents Protect Young

Many young animals have parents that protect them. To **protect** something is to keep it from danger. Parents may protect their young from the cold.

Visual Literacy Think of an animal. Draw how that parent protects its young.

meerkats

swans

Patterns Nature has many patterns. A **pattern** is something that repeats. Parents protect their young. They use their bodies to protect them. What patterns do you see on these two pages?

kangaroos

penguins

cats

Parents Teach Young

👆 INTERACTIVITY

Show how parents take care of their young.

Parent elephants teach their young different ways to act, or **behavior**. They show how to use their trunks. They show how to roll in mud. Mud keeps their skin safe from the sun.

Identify Underline two things parent elephants teach.
Circle the young in the pictures.

elephants

Young Stay Close and Make Sounds

Young stay close to a parent to stay warm. Young stay close to a parent to sleep. Young hold on to a parent to stay safe.

Young also help their parents. They cry and chirp to show they are hungry.

> ☑ **Reading Check** **Main Idea and Details** Underline one detail about the young.

koalas

birds

whales

Parents Help Young Learn

The grizzly bear cares for her cubs.

She feeds them and protects them.

The cubs learn to hide when in danger.

The black bear cares for her cubs.

She feeds them and protects them.

The cubs learn to climb trees to stay safe.

☑ **Reading Check** **Main Idea and Details**

Underline ways mother bears help.

Circle what the cubs learn.

black bears

grizzly bears

🟡 MAFS.1.NBT.2.3

Compare Numbers

The symbol > means more than.
The symbol < means less than.

Some animals live in groups.
You can use symbols to compare
the number of animals in each group.

Count The animals in each group.
Write the numbers in the boxes.

fish

turtles

Compare Write the correct symbol
in the sentence.

The number of fish is the number of turtles.

Find the Parents

What clues help us find a young animal's parent?

Look back through the pages. Find the parent that matches each of these young.

Show What You Found

You have found the young animals and their parents. Choose one. Draw the parent and young animal or make models from clay. Then write how the parent helps their young.

QUEST CHECK ✓ OFF

Career Connection

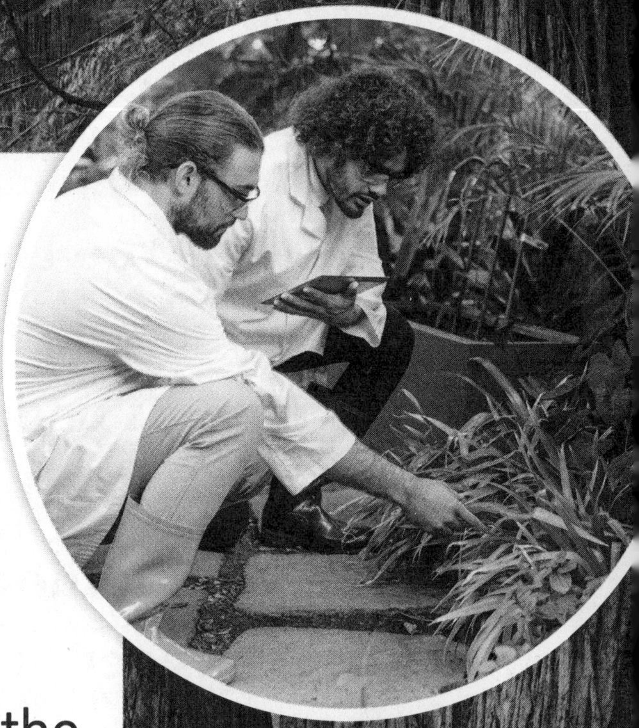

Nature Scientist

Nature scientists can study plants and animals. They can also study other things. A mushroom is part of nature. A rock is part of nature.

Some nature scientists work in the forest. Some work in the ocean. Others work in the mountains.

What parts of nature would you like to study?

The Essential Question
How are parents and their young alike and different?

Show What You Learned

Tell a partner what you learned about parents and their young.

Read each question and choose or write the best answer.

1. What pattern do you see in the photos?
   a. The young plant looks the same as the adult tree.
   b. The young plant grows and changes.
   c. The young plant is as tall as the adult.
   d. The seedling has more leaves.

2. Why would two plants that are the same age have a different number of leaves?

_____

_____

_____

3. How do young animals survive?
Use the word bank to fill in this table.

teach   cry   learn   protect   feed   stay close

Things Parents Do	Things Young Do

4. Grace claims that the photo shows a young zebra and its parent. Use evidence to support her claim.

_____

_____

_____

Read the scenario and answer questions 1–2.

Diego drew a model of a forest.

1 Which statement **best** describes what the model shows?

Ⓐ The model shows the weather in the environment.

Ⓑ The model shows how living things interact with the environment.

Ⓒ The model shows how rocks interact with the environment.

Ⓓ The model shows how the environment changes.

2 If a plant does not get enough sunlight, what will happen to the plant?

Ⓕ The plant will feel hungry.

Ⓖ The plant will not survive.

Ⓗ The plant will feel cold.

Ⓘ The plant will not change.

Read the scenario and answer
questions 3–4.

A dog has puppies. The
puppies grow and change.
The young dogs become
adult dogs.

3 How can you tell that these puppies are
related to their parent?

Ⓒ They make similar sounds.

Ⓓ They have similar fur patterns.

Ⓔ They have the same number of legs.

Ⓕ They have the same life cycle.

4 Describe what will happen next in the
young dogs' life cycles.

Ⓕ They will have offspring, or young,
of their own.

Ⓖ They will look different from their
parent.

Ⓗ They will stay the same size.

Ⓘ They will teach their young different
ways to act.

How do living things change as they grow?

Each material models part of a living thing. You will use these materials to observe the difference between the young and the parent.

Procedure

☐ 1. **Observe** the fishing line. This is like the quill of a young porcupine. Write what you observe in the table.

☐ 2. **Observe** the stirrer. This is like the quill of a parent porcupine. Write what you observe in the table.

☐ 3. **Observe** the pipe cleaner. This is like the stem of a young plant. Write what you observe in the table.

☐ 4. **Observe** the craft stick. This is like the stem of a parent plant. Write what you observe in the table.

Science Practice

You **observe** when you look closely at things.

porcupines

⚠ **Use care when handling pointed objects.**

Observations

Object	Observations
fishing line	
stirrer	
pipe cleaner	
craft stick	

Analyze and Interpret Data

5. **Explain** how a young porcupine is like and different from its parent.

6. **Explain** how a young plant is like and different from its parent.

How do scientists ask and answer questions?

Questions

Scientists ask questions about the world. Plants grow in soil. There is no soil in space. Scientists wanted to grow plants in space. They asked, "How might plants be grown without soil?"

Underline a question that scientists asked. Write a question you might ask about plants in space.

_____

_____

_____

_____

SC.1.N.1.1 Raise questions about the natural world, investigate them in teams through free exploration, and generate appropriate explanations based on those explorations.

Investigations

You investigate to for answers. Scientists investigated ways to grow plants without soil. Plants need nutrients from soil. Scientists added nutrients to water. They put the roots of some plants in the water. They observed how the plants grew.

Scientists shared what they learned. They explained how plants could grow in space without soil.

Circle what scientists investigated.

Underline how scientists investigated.

How do scientists make observations?

Your Senses

Scientists use their senses to observe the world. They can look, hear, smell, touch and taste. Then, they can tell others what they observed.

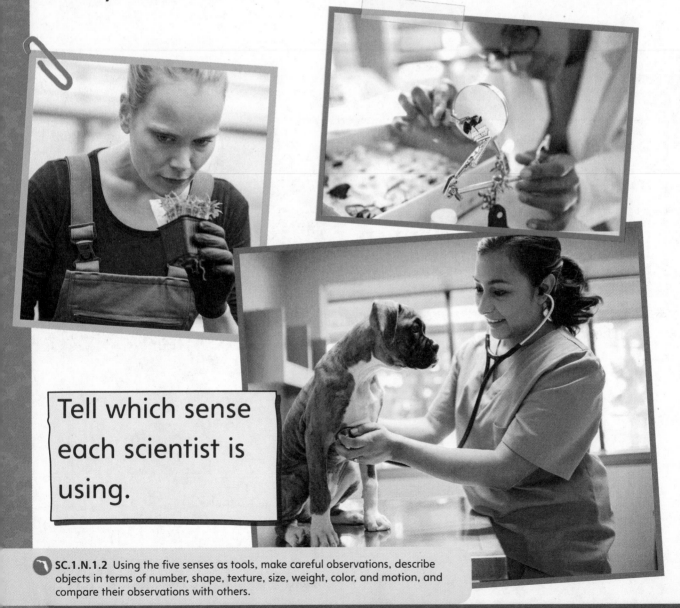

Tell which sense each scientist is using.

SC.1.N.1.2 Using the five senses as tools, make careful observations, describe objects in terms of number, shape, texture, size, weight, color, and motion, and compare their observations with others.

Tools

Scientists observe in many ways. Sometimes they use tools to observe. Scientists can use a thermometer to tell how warm something is. They use other tools to see small things better.

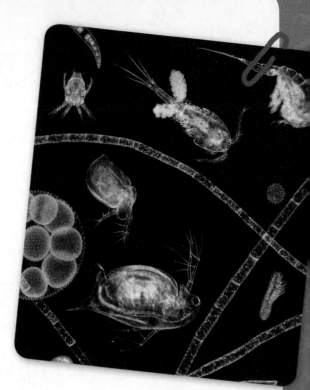

This scientist is looking at a drop of water with a microscope. How does the microscope help her?

_____

_____

_____

_____

How do scientists keep records?

Records

Scientists make observations during investigations. They record their observations. There are different ways to keep records. Charts, pictures, and illustrations are records. Journals and graphs are also records. Scientists use technology to record observations.

Circle the ways scientists can record observations.

SC.1.N.1.3 Keep records as appropriate - such as pictorial and written records - of investigations conducted.

Observations

Scientists make observations when they investigate. They share what they observe with other scientists. Other scientists do the investigation in the same way. Then, the groups of scientists can compare their observations. They find out if they got similar results.

Why should these scientists compare their observations?

How do scientists know if their results can be trusted?

▶ Evidence

Scientists want their work to be trusted.
They use evidence in their work.
Evidence is a set of observations that
shows something is most likely true.

parakeets

The picture shows blue
parakeets. A student states
that parakeets can be
different colors. How can
he prove his statement with
evidence?

_____

_____

_____

_____

Inferences

Scientists use their evidence to make inferences. Inferences are conclusions about an investigation.

In an investigation, scientists ask questions. They gather and record observations and evidence. Then, they make inferences to answer their questions.

A scientist studies bean plants. She gives one plant water and the other plant orange juice. She measures the height of each plant each day. She records her observations in the chart. What inference can the scientist make?

	Day 1	Day 3	Day 5
Water	10 cm	13 cm	17 cm
Orange juice	10 cm	11 cm	14 cm

Why do scientists repeat investigations?

Repeat Investigations

Scientists can make mistakes. A scientist might record a temperature incorrectly. This can lead to incorrect conclusions. Scientists may choose to do the same investigation, in the same way, many times. This helps scientists check their results. If they get the same result each time, then it is more likely their conclusions are true.

Underline why scientists repeat their investigations.

SC.1.N.1.2 Using the five senses as tools, make careful observations, describe objects in terms of number, shape, texture, size, weight, color, and motion, and compare their observations with others.

Groups at Work

Scientists often work in groups. Working in groups helps them share ideas. It helps them answer questions. Working in groups helps the scientists look at their work differently.

When scientists work together they can learn from each other. When scientists share what they know, they can figure out many different ways to solve problems.

Would you rather work with others or alone? Explain why.

Glossary

The glossary uses letters and signs to show how words are pronounced. The mark ′ is placed after a syllable with a primary or heavy accent. The mark ′ is placed after a syllable with a secondary or lighter accent.

adaptation (ad′ ap tā′ shən) A feature that helps a plant or animal stay alive where it lives. The green color of a frog is an **adaptation** that helps it hide.

behavior (bi hā′ vyər) A way of acting. Rolling in mud is a **behavior** of elephants.

compare (kəm pâr′) To tell how two things are alike. You can **compare** the shapes of two oranges.

contrast (kən trast′) To tell how two things are different. You can **contrast** the shapes of a banana and an apple.

environment (en vī′ rən mənt)) All of the living things and nonliving things in a place. A forest **environment** has trees, water, and soil.

erosion (i rō′ zhən) What happens when wind and water carry pieces of rock to new places. **Erosion** can change the shape of the land.

float (flōt) To stay on top of a liquid. Ice cubes **float** in water.

force (fôrs) A push or a pull. A **force** on a swing can make it move.

gill (gil) The part of a fish that helps it breathe underwater. The **gills** of a goldfish are near its head.

gravity (grav′ ə tē) A force that pulls objects toward Earth. **Gravity** causes rain to fall from clouds to the ground.

landslide (land′ slīd′) What happens when heavy rains and flooding push soil and rocks down a hill. The big storms caused a **landslide** to happen.

lava (lä′ və) Melted rock that pours out of a volcano and covers the land. **Lava** looks like a river of fire as it moves down the mountain.

leaf (lēf) The part of a plant that makes food. **Leaves** of some trees change color in the fall.

life cycle (līf′ sī′ kəl) The stages a living thing goes through during its life. An apple tree grows flowers during its **life cycle**.

living (liv′ ing) Things that need food and water, and that can grow and have young. A kitten is a **living** thing.

matter (mat′ ər) Anything that takes up space. A book is made of **matter**.

mimic (mim′ ik) To copy the way something looks or the way it acts. People **mimic** things that plants and animals do.

mineral (min′ ər əl) Nonliving things that make up rocks. **Minerals** in soil help plants grow.

moon phase (mün′ fāz) The changing shapes of the moon in the sky. The full moon is a **moon phase**.

motion (mō′ shən) The way an object moves. The **motion** of a swing is back and forth.

nonliving (non liv′ ing) Things that do not need food or water and that cannot grow or have young. A rock is a **nonliving** thing.

nutrient (nü′ trē ənt) Material in food that helps a body grow and stay healthy. Milk has many important **nutrients**.

ocean (ō′ shən) A very large body of salt water. Whales live in the **ocean**.

offspring (ȯf′ spring′) The young produced by parents. A puppy is the **offspring** of a parent dog.

pattern (pat′ ərn) Something that repeats. The changing shapes of the moon form a **pattern**.

protect (prə tekt′) To keep something from danger. A mother bear **protects** her young cubs.

root (rüt) The part of a plant that grows into soil. A tree **root** may be very deep.

rotation (rō tā′ shən) The spinning of an object. The **rotation** of Earth causes day and night.

scale (skāl) One of many hard plates that cover the skin of snakes and fish. Some fish have very colorful **scales**.

season (sē′ zn) A time of the year that has a certain kind of weather and amount of sunlight. Summer is my favorite **season** of the year.

sink (singk) To fall to the bottom of a liquid. A coin will **sink** in water.

soil (soil) Loose material that plants can grow in. Clay is a type of **soil** that holds a lot of water.

speed (spēd) How fast or slow an object is moving. An airplane moves at a very high **speed**.

star (stär) A large ball of hot gas in space. A **star** looks small because it is very far away.

stem (stem) The part of a plant that holds it up. The **stem** of a rose has sharp thorns.

sun (sun) The closest star to Earth. The **sun** is what makes the day sky bright.

sunrise (sun′ rīz′) What happens when the sun seems to rise in the sky in the morning. Many people get up each day at **sunrise**.

sunset (sun′ set′) What happens when the sun seems to set in the evening. Some animals like to hunt for food at **sunset**.

temperature (tem′ pər ə chər) A measure of how hot or cold something is. The **temperature** outside is high on this hot day.

texture (teks′ chər) How something feels to the touch. The rock has a rough **texture**.

weathering (weth′ ər ing) What causes rock to break apart or wear down. Wind and water can cause **weathering** of rocks.

weight (wāt) A measure of how heavy something is. A book has more **weight** than a pencil.

wetland (wet′ land′) An area of land that is covered with water. Ducks and frogs live in **wetlands**.

wildfire (wīld′ fīr′) A large fire that burns in a forest or field. A **wildfire** can happen when trees get very dry.

Index

Index

Illustrations

Peter Bull Art Studio; Sara Lynn Cramb/Astound US; Peter Francis/MB Artists, Inc.; Lauren Gallegos/C.A. Tugeau, LLC; Patrick Gnan/IllustrationOnline.com; Bob Kayganich/IllustrationOnline.com; Kristen Kest/MB Artists, Inc.; Erika LeBarre/IllustrationOnline.com; Matt LeBarre/Blasco Creative, LLC; Lisa Manuzak/Astound; Precision Graphics/Lachina Publishing Services; Geoffrey P Smith; Jamie Smith/MB Artists, Inc.; Mark Rogalski/Painted Words, Inc.; Mike Rothman/Melissa Turk; Ralph Voltz/IllustrationOnline.com

Photographs

Photo locators denoted as follows: Top (T), Center (C), Bottom (B), Left (L), Right (R), Background (Bkgd)

Front Cover: Alex Mustard/Nature Picture Library
Back Cover: Marinello/DigitalVision Vectors/Getty Images

FM

iv: Tanarch/Shutterstock; vi: Lucentius/iStock/Getty Images Plus; vii: Di Studio/Shutterstock; viii: Cineberg/Shutterstock; ix: Amble Design/Shutterstock; x: Andresr/E+/Getty Images; xii Bkgrd: Brian J. Skerry/National Geographic/Getty Images; xii TR: old apple/Shutterstock

T01

1: John Davis/Stocktrek Images/Getty Images; 2: Lucentius/iStock/Getty Images Plus; 5 Bkgrd: B.A.E. Inc./Alamy Stock Photo; 5 CR: Dennis Hallinan/Alamy Stock Photo; 6: Nata777_7/Fotolia; 7: Artur Marfin/Shutterstock; 8 B: Katrin Lillenthal/EyeEm/Getty Images; 8 Bkgrd: AlinaMD/iStock/Getty Images Plus; 9 CR: Lucentius/iStock/Getty Images Plus; 10 Bkgrd: Spiderstock/iStock/Getty Images Plus; 10 TR: Godrick/Shutterstock; 11: Lucentius/iStock/Getty Images Plus; 12: Terry Why/Photolibrary/Getty Images; 14 TR: AlinaMD/Shutterstock; 15 B: Westend61/Brand X Pictures/Getty Images; 15 TR: Sergii Broshevan/123RF; 16: PavleMarjanovic/Shutterstock; 17 Bkgrd: Aliaksei Lasevich/Fotolia; 17 BR: Lucentius/iStock/Getty Images Plus; 17 TR: Astrobobo/iStock/Getty Images Plus; 18 C: Luxx Images/DigitalVision/Getty Images; 18 TL: Lucentius/iStock/Getty Images Plus; 18 TR: Paola Cravino Photography/Moment/Getty Images; 19: Pandawild/Fotolia; 20: Aleksandr Belugin/Alamy Stock Photo; 22 TR: FotoMak/Fotolia; 22 C: Lucentius/iStock/Getty Images Plus; 22 BR: Snehit/Shutterstock; 23: Creative Travel Projects/Shutterstock; 24 TR: Lucentius/iStock/Getty Images, 24 BR Tatiana Popova/123RF; 25 TR: Tatiana Popova/123RF, 25 B: Bunya541/Moment Open/Getty Images; 28 Bkgrd: Standret/iStock/Getty Images Plus; 28 CL: AlinaMD/iStock/Getty Images Plus; 28 CR: Lucentius/iStock/Getty Images Plus; 29 BR: Erik Isakson/Getty Images; 29 TR: NASA Photo/Alamy Stock Photo; 30 BR: Claudio Divizia/Fotolia; 30 T: Pockygallery/Shutterstock; 34: Gay Bumgarner/Alamy Stock Photo

T02

36: Joe Vogan/Alamy Stock Photo; 37: Peter Horree/Alamy Stock Photo; 38 T: Di Studio/Shutterstock, 38 B: All Canada Photos/Alamy Stock Photo; 38 TC: Anton Foltin/Shutterstock; 38 BC: Kavram/Shutterstock; 41: Farbled/Shutterstock; 43: Bauman/Shutterstock; 44 Bkgrd: Checubus/Shutterstock; 44 BL: Giuseppe Porzani/Fotolia; 44 CR: MarcelClemens/Shutterstock; 45 BL: Becky Stares/Fotolia; 45 BL: Di Studio/Shutterstock; 45 BR: Di Studio/Shutterstock; 46: Jon Helgason/Alamy Stock Photo; 47 BC: Bruce Ellis/Shutterstock; 47 BL: Leon Werdinger/Alamy Stock Photo; 47 BR: Blickwinkel /Alamy Stock Photo; 47 TL: Di Studio/Shutterstock; 49: Wilsilver77/iStock/Getty Images; 50: Sergey Peterman/Shutterstock; 52: SunnyS/Fotolia; 53 BC: Di Studio/Shutterstock; 53 Bkgrd: Background All/Shutterstock; 53 CR: Kali9/E+/Getty Images; 54 BL: Adventure Photo/iStock/Getty Images Plus; 54 BR: Anton Foltin/Shutterstock; 54 TL: Di Studio/Shutterstock; 55 Bkgrd: Steve Bower/Shutterstock; 55 TR: M. Timothy O'Keefe /Alamy Stock Photo; 56: 123RF; 58 B: RWI Fine Art Photography/AlamyStock Photo; 58TR: Sumikophoto/Shutterstock; 59 BC: Di Studio/Shutterstock; 59 BR: PeteHendleyPhotography/iStock/Getty Images Plus; 60 BR: Bebo/Shutterstock; 60 TR: Enigma/Alamy Stock Photo; 61 BR: Keepics/Alamy Stock Photo; 61 TR: Joe Burbank/MCT/Newscom; 62 BR: Carl D. Benoit/Benoit Learning Services, LLC; 62 TR: Di Studio/Shutterstock; 64 BCR: All Canada Photos/Alamy Stock Photo; 64 Bkgrd: David Fettes/Cultura Exclusive/Getty Images; 64 BR: Di Studio/Shutterstock; 64 CR: Kavram/Shutterstock; 64 TR: Anton Foltin/Shutterstock; 65 Bkgrd: Saiko3p/Shutterstock; 65 TR: Eclipse Images/E+/Getty Images; 66 B: Walshphotos/Stock/Getty Images Plus; 66 T: KatieDobies/iStock/Getty Images Plus; 70 BC: PrairieArtProject/iStock/Getty Images Plus; 70 BR: Mayovskyy Andrew/Shutterstock

T03

72: Filmfoto03edit/Alamy Stock Photo; 74: Cineberg/Shutterstock; 76: RTimages/Shutterstock; 77: NASA; 78: Dimitrios/Shutterstock; 79: Dimitrios/Shutterstock; 80 Bkgrd: LeszekCzerwonka/iStock /Getty Images Plus/Getty Images; 81 TR: Quang Ho/Shutterstock; 81 BR Cineberg/Shutterstock; 82: YAY Media AS/Alamy Stock Photo; 83 BL: Denis and Yulia Pogostins/Shutterstock; 83 CL: Komkrit Preechachanwate/Shutterstock; 83 TCL: Ang Intaravichian/Shutterstock; 83 TL: Cineberg/Shutterstock; 86 Bkgrd: Stuart Aylmer/Alamy Stock Photo; 86 BL: Lawrence Roberg/Shutterstock; 86 CR: Wavebreak Media Ltd/123RF; 87 BR: Cineberg/Shutterstock; 87 TR: Kenileed/iStock/Getty Images Plus/Getty Images; 88: Cineberg/Shutterstock; 89 BC: Zahoor Salmi/Moment Open/Getty Images; 89 BL: James van den Broek/Shutterstock; 89 BR: Martin Harvey/Getty Images; 89 TR: Lzf/Shutterstock; 90 Bkgrd: Zdorov Kirill Vladimirovich/Shutterstock; 90 CR: Alvov/Shutterstock; 90 TR: Antonio Oquias/123RF; 92: Avalon_Studio/Vetta/Getty Images; 93: Africa Studio/Shutterstock; 94: Emyerson/iStock/Getty Images Plus/Getty Images; 95 Bkgrd: BrianAJackson/iStock/Getty Images Plus/Getty Images; 95 CR: Cineberg/Shutterstock; 96 BC: Jacek Chabraszewski/123RF; 96 BL: Kikor/Blend Images/Getty Images; 96 T: Sergey Novikov/123RF; 97 BR: Daniel Grill/Getty Images; 97 TR: Jetta Productions/Walter Hodges/Getty Images; 98: Cineberg/Shutterstock; 99 BL: 123RF; 99 BR: Dimedrol68/Shutterstock; 99 CR: Photosync/Shutterstock; 100 Bkgrd: Francesco Carta fotografo/Moment/Getty Images; 100 CR: Cineberg/Shutterstock; 101 Bkgrd: Tom Mareschal/Alamy Stock Photo; 101 TR: Sigrid Gombert/Cultura/Getty Images; 102 BR: Maram/Shutterstock; 102 T: Carlos Luis Camacho Photographs/Moment/Getty Images; 103 CL: Wavebreakmedia/Shutterstock; 103 CR: Hero Images Inc./Alamy Stock Photo; 106: Imagineerinx/Shutterstock

T04

108: Blickwinkel/Alamy Stock Photo; 110 TR: Amble Design/ Shutterstock; 112: Filipe B. Varela/Shutterstock; 113 Bkgrd: Dan Sullivan/Alamy Stock Photo; 113 TR: Gino Santa Maria/Fotolia; 114: VisionsbyAtlee/iStock/Getty Images Plus; 116 B: Sérgio Nogueira/Alamy Stock Photo; 116 CR: Fotolia; 117 B: Greg Vaughn/Alamy Stock Photo; 117 CR: Lucielang/Fotolia; 118 B: Rsooll/Fotolia; 118 BC: Amble Design/Shutterstock; 118 TR: KidStock/Blend Images/Getty Images; 119 Bkgrd: Bikemp/ Shutterstock; 119 TL: Amble Design/Shutterstock;122 Bkgrd: William Turner/DigitalVision/Getty Images; 122 CR: Amble Design/Shutterstock; 124 BL: Igor Plotnikov/Shutterstock; 124 BR: Marketa Mark/Shutterstock; 125 B: Hero Images/DigitalVision/ Getty Images; 125 TL: Amble Design/Shutterstock; 125 TR: Richard Griffin/123RF; 126: Matt/Fotolia; 127: Suponev Vladimir/ Shutterstock; 128 Bkgrd: Isabelle Bonaire/Fotolia; 128 TR: Christian Colista/Shutterstock; 129 BCR: Isabelle Bonaire/Fotolia; 129 CR: Mgkuijpers/123RF; 129 TR: Hummingbird Art/Fotolia; 130 BC: Amble Design/Shutterstock; 130 R: Admir Basic/Fotolia; 131 B: Steve Mann/Shutterstock; 131 TL: Amble Design/Shutterstock; 131 TR: Deb Campbell/Shutterstock; 132 TR: Blickwinkel/Alamy Stock Photo, 132 B: ImageBROKER/Alamy Stock Photo; 133: Thierry Van Baelinghem/Science Source; 136 Bkgrd: Chris Winsor/Moment/ Getty Images; 136 C: Amble Design/Shutterstock; 137: Greatstock/ Alamy Stock Photo; 138 BR: Ktaylorg/iStock/Getty Images Plus/ Getty Images; 138 TL: Amble Design/Shutterstock; 138 TR: Visual7/ E+/Getty Images; 140: CO Leong/Shutterstock; 141 BR: Yuriy Kulik/Shutterstock; 142: Adam Forster/EyeEm/Getty Images; 143 Bkgrd: Brian Hoffman/Alamy Stock Photo; 143 BR: Amble Design/ Shutterstock; 143 TR: Hero Images/Getty Images; 144 BR: Kwiktor/ iStock/Getty Images Plus/Getty Images; 144 TR: Douglas Klug/ Moment/Getty Images; 145 BR: Brais Seara/Moment Open/Getty Images; 145 TR: Peter Mulligan/Moment/Getty Images; 146 BC: Jim Cumming/Moment/Getty Images; 146 BR: Colleen Gara/ Moment/Getty Images; 146 TC: Amble Design/Shutterstock; 148 Bkgrd: Marco Pozzi Photographer/Moment/Getty Images; 148 BR: Amble Design/Shutterstock; 149 Bkgrd: CliqueImages/ DigitalVision/Getty Images; 149 TR: Hero Images/Getty Images; 150: Visual7/E+/Getty Images; 154: Herraez/iStock/Getty Images Plus/Getty Images; 155 : Herraez/iStock/Getty Images Plus/Getty Images

T05

156: Karel Gallas/Shutterstock; 157 BC: Andrii Rafalskyi/123RF; 157 BCR: miraswonderland/Fotolia; 157 BR: Dixi/Fotolia; 158 BC: Ben Queenborough/Shutterstock; 158 BL: renamarie/123RF; 158 BR: Henk Bentlage/Shutterstock; 158 TR: Andresr/E+/Getty Images; 160 CR: SzaszFabian Jozsef/Fotolia; 160 TR: denboma/Fotolia; 161: Chiyacat/Shutterstock; 162: Tofino/Alamy Stock Photo; 163 BR: Zoonar GmbH/Alamy Stock Photo; 163 C: Johannes Hansen/Alamy Stock Photo; 163 CL: Fotohunter/Shutterstock; 164 BL: Amophoto_ au/Shutterstock; 164 BR: Denis and Yulia Pogostins/Shutterstock; 164 C: Nattika/Shutterstock; 165 BC: Andresr/E+/Getty Images; 165 CL: Vladimir Wrangel/Shutterstock; 165 CR: Ger Bosma/ Moment Open/Getty Images; 165 TC: Trabantos/Shutterstock; 166 B: Igor Janicek/Shutterstock; 166 TCR: Andresr/E+/Getty Images; 169 CL: Elenathewise/Fotolia; 169 CR: Teemu Tretjakov/ Fotolia; 170 BC: Eric Gevaert/Fotolia; 170 Bkgrd: Krivosheev Vitaly/Shutterstock; 171 BL: PhilipYb Studio/Shutterstock;171 BR:

Viktor Kunz/123RF; 172 B: Nataliya Nazarova/Shutterstock; 172 TR: anrymos/Fotolia; 173 B: mikaelmales/Fotolia; 173 CR: Andresr/ E+/Getty Images; 174: Julija Sapic/Fotolia; 175 BC: EmiliaUngur/ Shutterstock; 175 BCL: WilleeCole Photography/Shutterstock; 175 BCR: wiktord/Shutterstock; 175 BL: Grigorita Ko/Shutterstock; 175 BR: tobkatrina/123RF; 175 CL: jarobike/Shutterstock; 175 CR: Grigorita Ko/Fotolia; 175 TL: Andresr/E+/Getty Images; 176: Milica Nistoran/Shutterstock; 177: Ralko/Shutterstock; 178: old apple/Shutterstock; 180 B: Sergey Krasnoshchokov/ Shutterstock; 180 CL: Debbie Steinhausser/Shutterstock; 180 TR: Rudmer Zwerver/Shutterstock; 181 BC: Andresr/E+/Getty Images; 181 CR: FloridaStock/Shutterstock; 181 TL: Gerrit_de_Vries/ Shutterstock; 182 B: Paul Farnfield/123RF; 182 T: Kelsey Green/ Shutterstock; 183 BL: aussieanouk/Fotolia; 183 BR: koldunova/ Fotolia; 183 T: idiz/Shutterstock; 184 BL: Johannes Lodewikus Van Der Merwe/123RF; 184 BR: Mark Bridger/Shutterstock; 185 B: 123RF; 185 TCR: Orhan Cam/123RF; 185 TR: Andras Deak/123RF; 186 B: Debbie Steinhausser/Shutterstock; 186 CR: Richard Seeley/Shutterstock; 186 TL: Andresr/E+/Getty Images; 187 BL: uwimages/Fotolia; 187 BR: trubavink/Fotolia; 188 Bkgrd: Polarpx/ Shutterstockj; 188 BR: Andresr/E+/Getty Images; 188 TC: Ben Queenborough/Shutterstock; 188 TL: renamarie/123RF; 188 TR: Henk Bentlage/Shutterstock; 189 Bkgrd: Sara Winter/Fotolia; 189 TR: WavebreakMediaMicro/Fotolia; 190 C: 816115/Shutterstock; 190 CL: Stocker1970/Shutterstock; 190 CR: AJF Natural Collection/ Alamy Stock Photo; 190 T: Jonathan Pledger/Shutterstock; 194: Scenic Shutterbug/Shutterstock

EM

196: Wavebreakmedia/Shutterstock; EM1: banprik/Fotolia; EM2 BR: Jetta Productions/DigitalVision/Getty Images; EM2 CL: A/ lvarez/E+/Getty Images; EM2 CR: Hero Images/Getty Images; EM3 BR: Peopleimages/E+/Getty Images; EM3 TR: Laguna Design/SPL/Science Source; EM4 BR: Robertcicchetti/iStock/ Getty Images Plus/Getty Images; EM4 TR: N. A. S./Science Source; EM5 BL: Craig Lorenz/Science Source; EM5 BR: Craig Lorenz/Science Source; EM6: Matt Cuda/Shutterstock; EM7: Yala/ Shutterstock; EM8: Blend Images/KidStock/Brand X Pictures/ Getty Images; EM9: Production Perig/Shutterstock; EM10: Mark Bridger/Shutterstock; EM11: Sumikophoto/Shutterstock; EM12: BrianAJackson/iStock/Getty Images Plus/Getty Images; EM13: Beboy/Shutterstock; EM14: Lawrence Roberg/Shutterstock; EM15: Debbie Steinhausser/Shutterstock; EM16: Avalon_Studio/Vetta/ Getty Images; EM17: AlinaMD/Shutterstock; EM18: RWI Fine Art Photography/Alamy

My Notes and Designs

Draw, Write, Create

My Notes and Designs

Draw, Write, Create